POSSESSIONS

New and Selected Poems
(1938–1985)

Other Books by Ben Belitt

POETRY

The Five-Fold Mesh (1938)
Wilderness Stair (1955)
The Enemy Joy: New and Selected Poems (1964)
Nowhere But Light (1970)
The Double Witness (1977)

PROSE

School of the Soldier (1949)

ESSAYS

Adam's Dream: A Preface to Translation (1978)

TRANSLATIONS

Four Poems by Rimbaud: The Problem of Translation (1947)
Poet in New York (Federico García Lorca) (1955)
Selected Poems of Pablo Neruda (1961)
Juan de Mairena and *Poems from the Apocryphal Songbooks*
   (Antonio Machado) (1963)
Selected Poems of Rafael Alberti (1965)
Pablo Neruda: A New Decade (Poems 1958–67) (1969)
Poems from Canto General (Pablo Neruda) (1969)
To Painting (Rafael Alberti) (1972)
Splendor and Death of Joaquin Murieta (Play by Pablo Neruda) (1972)
New Poems: 1968–70 (Pablo Neruda) (1972)
Five Decades: Poems 1925–1970 (Pablo Neruda) (1974)
Skystones (Pablo Neruda) (1981)
Pablo Neruda: Late and Posthumous Poems (1986)
Selections: F. G. Lorca, Eugenio Montale, Jorge Guillén, Jorge Luis Borges

POSSESSIONS

New and Selected Poems

(1938–1985)

BEN BELITT

David R. Godine

PUBLISHER · BOSTON

First published in 1986 by
David R. Godine, Publisher, Inc.
Horticultural Hall
300 Massachusetts Avenue
Boston, Massachusetts 02115

Library of Congress Cataloging in Publication Data
Belitt, Ben, 1911–
    Possessions : new and selected poems, 1938–1985.
    I. Title.
PS3503.E39P67   1986   811'.52   85-45969
ISBN 0-87923-626-4
ISBN 0-87923-633-7 (soft)

FIRST EDITION
Printed in the United States of America

For
Edith Barbour Andrews '41,
and the gift of remembering

Thanks are due to the following periodicals and publications in whose pages certain of the poems in this volume have previously appeared:
Poetry (Chicago), *The Virginia Quarterly Review, The Nation, The New Republic, Harper's Bazaar, Harper's Magazine, The Sewannee Review, The Georgia Review, The Southern Review, The Quarterly Review of Literature, The Bennington Review, Mundus Artium, Encounter* (London), *The New Yorker, Modern Poetry Studies, Salmagundi, Silo, The Poetry Review* (New York).

I am also grateful to the following Foundations for grants and awards which have, from time to time, freed me from other professional obligations and allowed me to devote my total attention to the writing of many of the poems which appear in this collection:
The Shelley Memorial Award, The Brandeis Creative Arts Award in Poetry, The Guggenheim Foundation, The National Endowment for the Arts, The Russell Loines Award for Poetry of the American Academy and Institute of Arts and Letters, Rockefeller Foundation Grant Bellagio (Italy), Yaddo Corporation, the University of Virginia, Bennington College.

Contents

III: Nowhere But Light (1964–1969)

IV: The Enemy Joy (1955–1964)

VI: The Five-Fold Mesh (1938)

I
New Poems: Possessions
(1977–1985)

*"If nothing is ever reborn,
what have we ever possessed?"*

Thoreau on Paran Creek

The freeze bears down
from this icy table-top in its mask of Kabuki
flour, and waits for the leavener's hand, intending bread.

Who shall provide for the wine and the loaves
in the hour of watery depredation—
the wounded water flayed with its alternate aftermath,
freezing and burning, the pond's skin laid open
in the thermal feasts of the fish, a cicatrix
stitched by a blind thermometer in bandages of sleet,
a Gadarene dragonfly
drying its fleeces and zincs on the stone
that was given to strike and the water, to drink?

    Thoreau, with sounding-line and chains,
      studied the bottom and dredged for an answer: *"Why
      do precisely these objects make up a world?"* he wrote
      in the salt of his thought,
      counting the bubbles, moving from cradle-hole and fault
      to the icy rosette at the center
      where Satan sat in the lobes and the glacial fat, hearing
      what Dante and Cotton Mather heard: the "diluvial crash"
      of the source, a booming of bees, and beyond,
      the breaking floe in the underground caves of the pond.

For nothing stands firm. Nothing keeps adamantine.
The water's block works downward
from opalescence, and the granite bores up
from a fiery hub that holds like the spokes of a wheel.
The solids sicken and mend, tangle
and loosen their lustre, hungry for metamorphosis.
The drowned demoniac sleeps in the lariat noose of the zero,
and Thoreau drifts in a berry-box.

                    His mind glistens,
disobedient, festive, a spinner.

              He pays out his plummet.

He listens.

                  (for Bernard Malamud)

Voyage of the Beagle

"If, as the poets say, life is a dream, I am
sure in a voyage these are the visions which
best serve to pass away the long night."

"Love of the chase is an inherent delight
in man."   —Charles Darwin

Hunting the old divinity of species
like Adam, he entered the peaceable kingdom
and saw at Galapagos a Chinese universe
supported by tortoises like an emperor's bibelot.

In his string-bag, over the chart tables, ear to the
ocean's floor, vomiting hardtack and gall,
he palpated the breathing of plates and the jostling
of continents, knowing nothing was finished—
Creation's sixth day, John's seven churches,
the conversions and the martyrdoms of Paul,
awaited their huntsman-interpreter—the bola's arc
flung from the fist of a Patagonian horseman
while the species still worked in the dark.

And gathered the delicate evidence on Alice's
tea-table in a dream of enormity
diminishing into the infinitesimal: first,
the bleeding of marble and waterspouts,
the clouds of Magellan, the moving and shaking of birds,
the Malthusian savage computing his global migrations
in surds and quadratic equations, Friday's
footprint vanishing into the rain forest; then,
a "rattling of stones" at the surf line, the lace-
makers knotting the atolls with fungus and coral,
the locusts of Luzan, the flea:

till all was Edenic diversity. The animal
mystery opened the way to the thirteen
mutations of spiders and mice, the finches'
metamorphoses, seventy-times-seven, including
the species named Charles, the eternal turned into
the heterogeneous, the hunted lay down with the hunter.

And the beached hypochondriac, indoors with the bread and the wine
of his pharmacopeia, opened a page of his journal.

(for Fred Burkhardt)

March Willows

This kindling of sacramental color—El Greco's
collapsed Count, a cadaver of haze, the green
of a closed or an opening grave,

fillets under the bent
wands, diagrams of fountains
rising and falling in faintly sinister gases,

phosphorus and pistachio—
yields to its seasonal Summoner as the diamond
yields to the shock of the diamond-breaker's hammer.

Now the daft
ward of a mad song hacks at her laces
and spins in her farthingale's balloon

under the deckle of a mortuary tree
past Kedron and Babylon,
dangling her weeper's hair

and combing the primitive
leaf in valences and serrations—
a stonecutter's sense of the willow

chiseled in airy chartreuse.
O the mind breaks this way and that, says the Summoner,
of its own crazed weight, shows an anvil's

underside, as the catamount's breath is seen
a moment between the thunderhead in the snow
and a glinting of evergreen,

while the whole of the willow breathes like a heart,
turning its rag-bag of leaves,
one way, leaden, like the meat of the olive,

the other way, yellow; and the lute in the stone
is heard in its lunatic sweetness
in a rising and falling of branches:

"O willow, willow!"

Sumac

*"I have seen
The incunabula of the divine grotesque."*
—Hart Crane

1.

The incunabula of the malign
that bloodies a summer with no obvious intent
to harm, raising the sumac's fist

on a gargoyle of waxes and berries,
a cockscomb with its brickdust wattles
bared, like maggots swarming,

is yet to come. Today
the malice is gone from the sumac. The delicate
balances drop either side the stem,

conservative as a fern, pinnate
and symmetrical. Night crawlers, creels,
a litter of cardboard containers and tins, the fishpoles, the boys,

the nude child with his pocketed father
booted in rubber and smelling of woodsmoke and plaid,
unreel in a cavern of leaves. The grass

is flashing with fishheads. Under the lilac's rot
the marauders sniff an illicit aroma:
acne and marijuana. Sinkers bobble. The bells: it is Sunday.

2.

That year of the suicide, the creek
took the print of her wretchedness: a hummock
of laundry face-down in the sumac's thicket,

and burned with habitual daisies. My dream
of the Drum Room returned,
with its bonfire of rawhide and brasses, its

captain's insignia glowing alongside the drumsticks,
stacked sheet music, gold braid,
the boy in the hangar too late for the evening formation,

7

dazed in the Drum Captain's arms, watching the sleepy
parade, while the sticks whirred with primitive messages;
and under the tympanum's hoop,

the crossed cords on the drum,
the man's hand guided the child's to the sheltering place at the center
where the sumac opened its pouch in the leafy graffiti.

3.

All reads so easily now—the doorposts and plate glass of a
village with their initials and capital letters, a trout's
back seen through the gloss

of a signpainter's fantasy. They say
all that is needed to say. "There's
the greengrocer's logo; there, under the bar-lights,

The Villager's comic cartoon; a spaceman's balloon
in a glinting of newsprint; the spine
of a split book; the poem." They say what is common to all

and lives again in the noon
of the near and beholdable, as though nothing
could ever grow darker. Yet there

at the summit, in the sumac's
topmost corona, the cone of the summer cockade prepares
its swarthy declension again: feathers and spearheads

unscathed in a jungle of asterisks, pinpoints, suspension
dots—Lilliput's minuscule orchards written
on air in phosphor and punk with a Fourth of July sparkler.

4.

Why should I see you today in a pantry-door's
brass in the Orphanage kitchen?
Little sister, I was wiping the paste with a chamois under the platters

when suddenly you were there
with your gift of a breadcrust hidden away in your bloomers.
A bell shocked us awake. We stepped out on the steel.

of a fire escape suspended together at three in the morning.
We looked down to the court where we dangled our legs
for a movie. You were

under the trees gathering pitch on the playground—
the green scum banding the bark for the midsummer
plague of the caterpillars. You were pasting

cutouts in my copybook. We stared
through the orphanage gates at a trophy of paper: *"Mother,
come closer!"* We waited. And *"Stay!"* we said. *"Stay!"* Then fifty years later,

jailed in your fears, an offended spectator, she came
through the sumac, the reddening grass and ailanthus, to your cancerous
condominium window. A telephone rang you away.

5.

Which way to the sumac? The Indian tanners
are softening their leathers somewhere with its acids and chalks,
the bog-walkers, rooting for pitcher-plants, poison their shins

with its venoms. I remembered Chichén—the jade jaguar's heart flung
with the necklace of claws in a grain-god's *cenote*,
the Vesuvial bronzes and blacks of implacable fruitage—

all the warring mutations, benign or malignant by turns, that work in the
species, devising a wart knobbled over, a tumor, a pollen to steep
for the tea of a rabbit in waistcoats, a devil's caduceus:

mahogany, laurel, or sugarbush—which?
They say that Proserpine passed with her pomegranate through a column
of sumac to kindle her bloody flambeaux with its berries. Now

all the torches are lit in the atrium. The landscape is dangerous.
In the distance the gatherers go in their nightly guerrillas
mining the creeks of a village, in their broken

fatigues screened with leaves like chain lightning, intent
upon pillage. They wait where the roads and the bridgeheads begin.
    Underneath,
in the branches and pennants, the sumac's grenade is ready.

6.

The marauders move in. They lean toward the terrible fruitage, grope
for the ring in the gunpowder, feel how it bleeds to their bite
like the pith of the pomegranate, pierced.

                                    They pull the pin.

Walker

"*Death to the Lady said*
While she to dancing measures still
Would move . . ."
                    —Léonie Adams

Stalled in a country house, in an angle of her walker,
her gaze, grown useless and exigent, holds a threshold,
a doorframe, a quadrant of Candlewood Mountain.

                                        On the baize
background of her longing, a thought peaks and explodes,
vanishes in string-bags and pockets:

"Today I just had to get out for a walk—"

The world offers no loving concessions. In the peaceable
kingdom, blackberries aim their inks in an open portcullis,
armed with a cockerel's spurs.

"—only as far as the clearing," she thinks.

The V of her walker descends and descends.

                                        She has left
the interior world of staircases, rag rug, quotidian
obstacle races. Matted with accident, she flattens the weedy
largesse of her passing and levels the meadow in wedges.

"Those are the mowers of Marvell," she says. "Those,
the child's valedictions, an autumnal acrostic of
leaves. I remember the violet-gatherers, the horns and the hares
of a festival, the runners with lots, the gleaners, the sowers,
the sheaves. And those are the grapes and the shears."

Uncaring, the summer's exuberance breaks like a surf on her
passage. She veers in the salt and contingency, spinning an invisible
mariner's wheel, a figurehead rising and falling in chicory: rides
over the paddles and flails of a threshing floor, last looks and
dismemberings, flaws in a lost cornucopia.

                                The vise of her walker
is blossoming.

            "I see brackets of grapeleaves," she says, "a sundial's

planchette and a whimsical compass's point spelling out
messages, thunderheads printing the air . . ."
a dancer, prosthetic in iron, gasping with steam on the
cloth, measuring time for the dithyramb and moving the chorus.

"I have come to dance out the quarrier's joy on the flint
of an age's abandonment."

                The gods in the walking-machine
beckon to her from the clearing.

                        She enters the ring of the dancers.

She is theirs.

Annunciation to Joseph

Looking up from the bole
on the ringleted carpenter's block,
the incense under the saw,
he paused as the blade buckled and a sunburst
opened an improbable fan in its blinding serrations.

And thought:
>   All goes as it must.
A fragrance of resin and camphor sweetens the sawhorse.
The ruler's edge measures the place where the stylus
passed over, to a decimal fraction,
the part vanishes into the whole, wedge matches wedge
and confirms the plumb line's vibration.
The reckoning is just.

Then how is it everything goes so abstract?
The blueprint trembles with musical signatures,
and wherever the balancing bubble has lain
an angel works in the grain,
The posts of the temple are moved (as the prophet has said)
and the saw's tooth snaps on the knot.

What should a sawyer's apprentice
know of the marvelous, or an angel require
of him? One beam weighs down the other.
The roof rises over the inn and the stable,
the pedestal leaps from the plinth.
Shall the thing that is building rise on a palpable loss?
The journeyman has his reward, the builder is worthy his hire.

I am moved by no journeyman thing.
I smell dung on the terebinth
floor, and the ox's stall curves like a cradle.
The arches reject the seams of the pillar in their
Roman similitude and
pull to a point, as if to outdistance creation
and gather all under their wing.

Something is building.
The consort of Solomon calls from the garden:
the godson awakes with the bridegroom
and the virgin lies down with the bride.

13

Shall they join what the axe and the hammer never hewed
out of cedar and granite?
Does the whole of the carpenter's subtlety end and begin
with a cross?

A carpenter's son does well to be wary.

Hail, Mary!

Possessions

(for Nick Mayer)

1.

The shameful last shovelful
that forced the burial doors
on all that pharaonic junk: a boy-king's rumpus room
of funerary boats, inlays of faience and ebony
for a fowler's boomerang, long-necked amphorae,
wig boxes, gold-leaf pectorals, dismantled chariot wheels—
the toy-rooms of Tutankhamen—

and there, under his three sarcophagi,
the dispossessed possessor in his headstrong barricade,
no longer Nilus's god, but a violated
child, cross-armed and disemboweled, stockpiled in the silt,
his abdomen scoured with palm wine, myrrh, papyrus,
his cheekbones carven with spices and verdigris,
holding the flail and the crook of the Heliopolitan
under a top-heavy crown, his eyes like ankhs
in the gilt and lapis lazuli, staring the tomb-robbers down.

2.

"I waked to my perishing things,
ownerless and provisional, in a field of bric-a-brac.
I heard the tumblers yield
to a safecracker's fingertips while the despoilers
took possession, crowding the Theban desert
with turquoise and chalcedony, pendants, gold falcon-heads, baboons—
all the inviolable iconography of transcendence:

'Mother,' I said, 'Mother:
I thought to come with my footstool and my abacus
as in the nonage of my schooldays, whistling for Anubis.
It is frightening to wake in a windowless broom-closet
of a crypt where even my playthings turn into menacing attributes
and cutthroats and curators covet my souvenirs from Memphis.
Where is the godhead safe, if not at the pyramid's point—
Osiris's honeycomb
sealed by the goldsmith and caulked with shipmaker's resin?

What do we bring to the gods if not corn from the banqueter's table,
linens from Karnak, the artifacts and baggage of our status?
If nothing has followed us there, if
nothing has stirred in the desert but some nondescript intruder,
if an Englishman from Cairo with a writ for our arrest
lays violent hands on a Pharaoh's portion, after the long hiatus—
if nothing is ever reborn,
what have we ever possessed?' "

3.

Midwinter in the Firehouse. The Creek prints
its double parchment in the icy splinter-play: the upper
scroll of the Falls on the bottommost scroll of the Falls:
a midrash of hieroglyphs.

        A fortress's thickness divides
the furnace-room from the freeze on the other side of the wall.

In the cellar's glacial cement
I breathe in the gas of the dehumidifier,
count calories in the knocking of the furnace, dream semiotic
pageants, trace fractions of oil on the arrowhead of the gauges. I stash
what I can in the vanishing sound of the bells.
I ready the trash.

        Overhead, at the peak of the roof—
the pyramid's point where the architect carved from the block
a sundeck for a tentative sun-worshiper—I hear the tomb-robber's
hammer tap at my crypt of books. I count my Egyptian
possessions:

        Alberti's angels and doves in the pane of a coffee-table;
Lorca, Neruda, Siqueiros; Motherwell cutting acidulous prisms
in metals and piercing the walls with a pope's fenestrations;
Rocky, my Firehouse familiar, with a pugilist's paws and panache;
some chimerical keepsakes a tourist might filch from a flea market—
glass paperweights, millefleurs, or a dandelion's pinwheel
in plastic; sarapes; some Mexican gesso; Chacmol
recumbent, looking over his shoulder toward Uxmal
or Palenque; a Peruvian drummer in whimsical candy-stripes; my
steel file of duplicate documents—all the rubbish
of Thoth and Tutankhamen, with that glint of the private

and poignant—Andromeda held in the loop of the void like a zodiac:
a collector's vagaries metamorphosed into possessions
I would heap at the door if I could, to interpret
my lost predilections and repeat my identity.

Nicky and Judy and Eddy and Robert and Dusty—
deliver my things from the vandals!

The Creek jostles its darknesses under the ice.
Below is a roaring, a grating of angles and edges, a slobber,
a drowning.

The boiler-room readies its column of blood in the shaken
thermometer and sets forth on the torrent.

What have we ever possessed?
I wait for the tomb-robbers.

in the salt meander,
      -back nuzzling the sea-holly
       ich of coppery bubbles, chain mail, saliva,
repeating a sponge's disguises,
speaks for the animal mystery.

It puzzles like scrimshaw,
whittling its bulk to a mote for the
pouch of a slingshot. It works in the watery waste
where the particles enter,
calls us to dance with Democritus,

and points to the plummeting
center. Below, in the lair of the
octopus, Peter quarries his drowning cathedral, the polyp
readies its gargoyles and waterspouts,
pools gather like isinglass,

Leviathan basks by the reefs,
plane over plane in the plankton,
confounding the Comforters, reflecting, reversing, refining,
turning substance to essence, being to imminence,
basalt and mica to ether:

and above, in the void of that other
Beginning, floats the stone that we
read by, the mariner's or the sibyl's, that mimics the tides and
the solstice and casts back the parched
and nocturnal in its freezing redundance—

the moon of the gypsy diviner
who measures by crescents and quadrants, writes
in cartographer's chalks in the desert where the astronaut's boot,
the whips of the punishing Pharaohs,
the charioteers, all splinter at last.

Brutto Tempo: Bellagio

(Lake Como)
(for Gina Werfel)

The eye and its alpenstock cannot force their way
back to the passes—that tiara of peaks for a storm-king, stainless
steel on majolica moist from the artisan's

brushstroke. Today, all is the mash
of a hack's mistranslation: terza rima, chiaroscuro,
gravure on the slopes, rooftiles in a hachure

of cloudy serrations like a tortoise's armature or the
underside of a shell, a rotting away
of the pear blossoms, implacable ash and decay—

all the forfeits of outline, dimension, enclosure,
a perspective of circles and cycles for a Dantean parable,
a purgatorial heath for Doré.

Nothing remains of the Village: only pockets
in packets, cauldrons and fissures, as though
a lake smoldered and broke in the fog

in a rubbish of cypress and ochre. Yet
below, the boats still stand unscathed in the scatter—spent wicks
in a spindle of hurricane glass,

in the pewter and tin of the coves. In the workshops of Como
silk boils on the looms like milkweed and dandelion
seed. Demogorgon has breathed

on the glass. The volatile life
of the imminent—self-loss and self-manifestation—
wrestle like opposite presences,

thigh to thigh, for the gift of a blessing. But here
in the pit, nothing prodigious
acknowledges the workings of providence. There is

only Gina, come down from the Villa,
her outrageous umbrella striped like a medicine ball
for the balancing act of a poodle,

to toil in the clottings of fog and the world's
suppuration, bearing her paint box, a scrap of stretched
canvas, an improbable easel—a vulnerable

mote in the wind and the void. Her brush's point churns
in a plasm of oil, ascending, descending,
preparing a lane to the passes

till the wet of the canvas is covered and the color is total.
Peak after peak reassembles. Her alpenstock strikes for
the palette's horizon and holds firm on the glazes

and she waves back to us from the summit.

*Esmiss Esmoor

"God si love."

Having no mariner's thumb for navigational cunning,
no wish to shore up a bowsprit with the blind eye
and décolletage of a figurehead, I am
reduced to this: a tripper, aging in cardigan,
nursing a pittance of beef broth for its moment of
warmth, decked on the leeward side, sailing for England.

A needle works in the shrouds and my
deckchair yaws like a spinnaker.

          I go voyaging
over caverns and courtrooms and mosques, spelunker
of nightmares and marriages, while a voice
in the void thrashes and settles without echo or issue—
bo-oum and *bo-oum* and *bo-oum*—in a
troglodyte's language.

          For a moment,
all sways like the fan of a punkah. A gavel
smashes on teak, like a battle-mace.

          It is the
picnic in Marabar again—a rapist's excursion
to a jungle of Indian courtesies and juridical
voices, or a god's day of overturned boats,
fetuses drowning in semen, nausea, depression. All
spins in an ocelot's widening eye, and grows feral.
I step from the sponge and the cloth of my sandals
and a young man repeats his Mohammedan formula:
You are one of us!, bowing in crumpled madras.

One of us? One of us? *What should I know
of the Ninety-Nine Attributes?*

          I faint
in the mangroves and toddy palms. I claw in the dark of the cave.
I ready the flint and the straw for a matriarch's
sacrifice. My own get torments me. I lessen and lessen

(Mrs. Moore, disavowing all loyalties and divinized by her Hindoo admirers as "Emiss Esmoor," turns her back on the compounding disasters of her visit to India, and dies en route to England, having accomplished nothing.)

in a world of subalterns. I am naphtha, nothingness,
carrion. I quail in the fetor of rank
copulation, see sweat on a triangle furred like
a bat, a Solomon's seal on the pubis of Priapus,
the horse of Apocalypse baring a uvula
scorched by a planet's explosion:

bo-oum and *bo-oum* and *bo-oum* . . .

My broth goes to vinegar. No one will lift
a beneficent finger to steady the suppliant's cup
or beckon me back to my father's verandah.

The fan will not yield to the weight of the winnower.

There is nothing to breathe on the Bay.

Yet I sail

toward the son of the blessing as though all were made one
in retributive havoc and innocence: the sea-lanes
to England, and the pestilent ash of the Ganges.

Heartbeat by heartbeat, I emerge from the cave
of libidinous taint on the quick of my footsoles,
empty of being.

Buddha laughs from the Bo Tree of Gya,

and behind him, the night-hag, the umbilical boy, and the saint.

A wasp stitches his way through the mandala,
writing all down with the sexual bone of his stinger.

The air smells of honey and gossamer, essence of wormwood and camphor.

The web widens from ocean to ocean.

(Homage to E. M. Forster)

Graffiti

Till all was in readiness:

There, in my vandal's dream,
the straphangers sagged under the lictor's festoon
of their nooses and the coaches bored through the tinder.

The sound was a jackhammer's sound, the sizzle
of flanges and bits in a gun barrel. The light was peacock-blue—
blue as the tossing of flares in a troughing of water or
the glinting of spice in a urinal, blue as the night-light
in a crescent of vanishing corridors—cornflower
and chicory blue on the standing tooth of vermilion
that strikes the sum of the burning.

Spray-gun in hand,
in the tomb-robber's darkness, I dreamed of my doubled
initials: a jungle liana of loops in a gangster's cartouche, a beanstalk
of curlicues, calligrams, cave scribbles branching flintily out
to the roof like smoke from a pistol.
I tasted the charge
of the rails to the roots of my nostrils, and the tunnels erupted
in a hashish explosion.

There were the platforms
and carriages, the time-lapse ascents of the pods for a giant,
branching over and under: the reds and the greens of a tapeworm
cartography stinting the windows with a knifegrinder's
emery hiss, the guillotines venting their closures and
human discharges, the placenames, the stations . . .

So I struck with the
felt of my marker. I struck. I struck at the windows. I struck
under the bulbs through the flying chromes and aluminum
with the mark of my lifetime's rejections till all
turned to neon.

There was my name with its starving
imprimatur! All glowed with my signature—
the studs of the girders, the crossties, the gritty enamels,
the sheath on the heart of the diesels.
It said
B over B over B over B over B, in the code
of a banker's equivalence.

23

"You know me," I wrote with my spray-gun.
"You know me, you mandarin wards of the bitch-goddess,
gatekeepers there at the change-boxes, flashing your semaphores:

> *'This far and no further! He gets only as far*
> *as the spokes of the turnstile! Close off the exits,*
> *the fireman's poles to the kiosks,*
> *the pornographer's heaven of nipples*
> *and penises!*
> > *The subject is armed and dangerous!' "*

But already the walls blazed with
bison and horn. My downstrokes and capital
letters were scored into room after room of the coven, slashed
with the inks of my underground rages, the singular vowel
of my losses.
> It said
I it said I it said I it said I.

> That way,
I thought, it could be done. That way
my vengeance could work in the manholes, Jocanaan's vow
could carry my manifestations to the barns at the end of the run.
Never mind the comings and goings two stories above
in the streets! Never mind the nightsticks and badges,
the comedy chase of the transit police!

> That way, the signs
could be carved into the domes of the blinded macadam,
the caravans, seared with my brand, drink deep at the railyards in the iron
savannahs, the Alexandrian libraries re-arise from the flames
and the whole of the canon be one.

Crossing the Ice: Acapulco

The children are flying,
non-poisonous,
tentacular, in bladders
and blisters of nylon, Mary Poppins umbrellas,
over a groundglass Pacific, dangling
amphibian thighs as though weighing the thread
of their altitude
in the pans of their testicles.

Below,
the tours gather sunburn and coconut oil, bubble like
squids from the lobbies and discotheques, clot
and decaffeinate on the boomerang
curve of the shorefronts.

Tamed to a diver's
cliché, hazard rehearses its gig
on the cliffs. Flea markets jostle
the swarming costeras. A pony barouche coasts in its harness
of colored balloons.

It is time for the toucans, the mechanical sewer rats,
T-shirts inscribed with the last metamorphic declensions
of Ovid, a daiquiri slush
of erotica feathered with green and magenta.

It was hard
to live under an icicle's point with a snowblower's rectitude,
freeze to a halt and tunnel a lane from Vermont
to this Walden for surfeiters.

Now the horsemen of Cortés
debouch on a fairway of chicklets. The mendicant mothers
sleep sound in a midnight of sandals.
Under
a sunset's tortilla
I balance my way home to my perils
on a black-and-white ice-cake, with Eliza and Lillian.

II
The Double Witness
(1970–1976)

. . . this want of witness in brute nature . . .
—Gerard Manley Hopkins
(Letter to W. R. Dixon)

. . . reckon but, reck but, mind
But these two; ware of a world where but these two tell, each
off the other . . .
—Gerard Manley Hopkins,
"Spelt From Sibyl's Leaves"

Xerox

The original man lies down to be copied
face down on glass. He thinks what it is
to be other than he was, while the pilot light
goes garnet, a salamander's eye
blinks in the camera's cave, green burns like the skin
of the water seen by a surfacing swimmer:
and the moving and shaking begin.

What must it be, to be many? thinks the singular
man. Underneath, in the banked fluorescence, the rollers
are ready. A tarpaulin falls, A humming of flanges
arises, a sound like rail meeting rail
when power slams out of the fuses. A wick explodes
in the gases—and under the whole of his length
the eye of the holocaust passes.

And all that was lonely, essential, unique
as a fingerprint, is doubled. Substance and essence,
the mirror and the figure that printed the mirror,
the deluge that blackened creation and the hovering pigeon
with the leaf's taste in its beak
are joined. The indivisible sleeper is troubled:

What does it mean to be legion?
he cries in the hell of the copied. The rapists, the lovers,
the stealers of blessings, the corrupt and derivative
devils, whirl over the vacant emulsion.
The comedian peers from the brink and unsteadily copies
its laughter. The agonist prints its convulsion.
Like turns to like, while the seminal man on the glass
stares at his semblance and calls from the pit of the ink:

Forgive our duplicity. We are human
and heterogeneous. Give us our imitations!
Heart copies heart with a valentine's
arrows and laces. The Athenian dream and the adulterers paired
in the storm tell us the mirrors are misted. The whole of our art
is to double our witness, and wait. And the original man on the plate
stands and steps down, unassisted.

Kites: Ars Poetica

The innocents have come to make their cast
in the sky, fishing upside-down
and flying heraldic signs, Chinese
or Euclidean, with parallel squares
and dotted balsa lines
in vanishing tissue paper—
heart-shapes, shields,
or whatever their breath
can bend to a crossbow of twine
or cut in armorial fields
and make fly—

like that other caster of lightning
paying out bamboo, watching the reel and the spinner
break electrical water,
touch a key in the creel
and blaze for the Philadelphian
with the shock of the trout's phosphorescence—

till, somewhere between the helicopter's star
and a vanishing point in the sea,
I feel myself go up,
unreeling aerial rigging out of my side
and shedding a helix of thread,

an invisible top in the air

a spider climbing the light—

till the whole web bells, and goes tight—

and I am flown by the kite.

Swan Lake

The swan, a stylist, born to the posture ᴄ the question mark
and the bishop's mitre—
balletic, episcopal, unsentimental,
a hater of Tchaikovsky, inadvertently
settling his calm posterior like a tutu, fixing his seedy
eyeball like a lorgnette in the garbage and crumbs—
is nobody's accompanist. He leads
a hard flotilla in half a V,
parting the cattails, makes a fist
of his breastbone, aims the carroty wax of his beak,
and smashes the flat of the pond
till nothing is seen in the scum
but the doubled hose and the albino spur of his rump.

Never having read
Ovid's *Metamorphoses,* he is content
with the basic changes of the uxorious loner:
his cygnets making chevrons in the swamp,
training for puberty, drifting like crumpled carbon paper
with the letters showing faintly through the smudge,
pica on *elite,*
till white burns through the hump
and all that was ordinary turns exceptional.

The swan is unreflective, opposing the hard outline
to the blur,
casting a classical image like the Parthenon
in an Ionian ambiguity of pomp,
oblivious to imagery, equivalent
only to itself. Those who have known his anger,
know the alternate sides of a coin: tenderness
and homicidal hate—
the beer-drinking family man and the fighter
cocked with a trigger's violence
showing the naked triangle of his uvula
parted to the gullet under a bony bulb, like the Guernica horses—

as the whole contrivance hisses and advances,
saying:
> *Bastards! Bastards! Bastards!*

                        And tacks round
and stands its ground.

The Repellant

(for Melissa Hayden)

Coming to dinner with the ballerina, in that improbable
weather of swans and necromancers, hunters
of holocaustal birds, scenarios in Ukrainian
magenta, we climbed the spas and stables,
rose in the yeasty heat of Saratoga,
found the place appointed in the fable—a
crossbow in a coronet of feathers—
and entered the open circle of the dancers.

Behind us, on the nether levels, blind
guests to the symposium of summer
sped on their simultaneous errands—the centaur's
stations in a universe of horses
stretching their charmed necks in a jockey's
collar of roses; Hassidim in bicarbonated water
singing in mineral gases, Victorian gingerbread,
Norwegian spruces, pizzas, Goldberg variations.

And then: the dancer's house, with its aquarian
windows clearing the trees' scrim, its birdbath
stance and unemphatic lawns, its pathway
like a tutu of begonias and nasturtiums; and
parallel to the sky, five candles of ultraviolet
repellant, cold cartridges of phosphorescent neon, traps
of mercurial darknesses and lights, magnetic
fields subtle with mosquitoes come to dance.

We talked, over the meat and flowers, while a darkening
world emptied the picture windows and blackened the colors,
dividing outer and inner, the propitious and the evil.
Only a blank pane, and the pathos of our
human conversation—breakable, incessant, over-eager—
defined our dances from the dance of the mosquitoes:
the intriguer's infinitesimal banquets of blood,
from the love-feasts of a night's improvisations.

Beyond, in the starlit vault, the stingers swarmed,
ringing the candles in the revels of Oberon,
building quasars for the firebird and the swan,
pylons of acid and ink colored like

the venom in the jellyfish's blister,
the incendiary's gentian violet,
zodiacs of peacock oils and pinks,
attracting and repelling, leading the dancers on,

as the whole house trembled in the dice-cup of a gambler.
The mosquitoes arched their backs on the sleeping village
and entered the burning nimbus, winding and unwinding
their skeins. The Prince of Darkness moved through the
Athenian wood, calling the flowers by name: *Pease-Blossom,
Oxslip, Mustard-Seed.* And the Pythoness,
blazing with lice, at the spindle of creation,
smiled at her creaturely void, watching the colors dwindle.

And spat into the cinders.

Double Poem of the World's Burning

1. *"Ah, Sunflower!"*

Preparing for that presence, the pod
chose a man's height, set its cleats in the leaves
like a steeplejack, scribbled its target of ovals,
and rose to eye level.

Climbing a profile of gardens, a Nimzo-Indian
chessboard of vegetables, villages, rock with its pollen
of lichen, the sunflower steadied its petals in zodiacal
yellow, and struck like a clock.

All the world's plenty, all the brazen particulars—a bull's-eye
of seeds with the pips pointing down into chain-metal, an obsidian
disk bulging with roe like a carp—took on the hardness
of Chinese enamels

and opened its perfect meniscus. Then the terrible
heaviness began—the failing of bronzes, the hasp at the sunflower's
center breaking away, a fading of planets, eclipses, coronas,
the falling and falling away of the petals—

Time's total weariness, the terrible weight in the sun—all
that hammers at darkness and glows like the baize of the table Van Gogh
saw at Arles, in the cornfields and candles: a madman painting the night till
the sky was delivered again to the crows.

2. *Glare: Atlacomulco*
"And his raiment was white as the light."

The invisible life that sleeps in the grossness of things
and feeds on the bulk of the world
bringing substance and weight and degree—

the tumescence
that traces a thread in the loins, to the swamp
of our human duration

and insists on the blood and the bone of our presence—
shows the world's burning,
turned low, like the flame in the bell of a lamp.

Blue as acetylene, it waits
at the furthest edge of the morning, a transparency
holding a bird and a steely horizon:

the water repeats it: gunmetal on pewter,
pewter on ultramarine,
doubling the universe, spilling the colors

and shapes of a season
on the rubble and flint of a planet, crowding
the leaf to its uttermost margin, filling the spaces,

till nothing is latent, nothing withheld or unnameable:
the spike of the cactus, the fuse in the tulipan, the sun
at its zenith, lie flat on the plane of the sky like an armorer's anvil,

and the fullness of time is complete. Then
that burning away of the air, as the glowing erasure
of limit begins: a glare

on the claws and the cusps of poinsettia
tracing the heat's line with a solderer's iron, petal for petal—
a talon of ash

on a talon of smoking vermilion, forcing the fire at the center
to bloom on the edges and smolder like metal,
scoring the water

with hurrying scallops cut into friezes and crystals,
blowing the coal of the world's
calefaction till the unbinding of matter is done,

the visible turns into the invisible,
the invisible, into an omen, and out of the hearthbed of summer
the suffering hedonist stands forth—

the Man who came eating and drinking, whose clothing was "white as the light,"
lifting his skull's lamp to the darkness and saying: *I am the Light
of the world!*—to deliver himself to the Romans.

The Guanajuato Mummies

The body of those deaths is given us now (the child
guide says, for a peso) by a trick of mineral gases—the stale
exhalation of silver and the weight of the quarries—
with a potter's underground skills. In the cupboard's glass
plate stacking the corridor, the re-arisen
recumbents, clown-white on their jawbones, disgorging
a petrified vomit, are erect now.
                    Parodists
of perpetuity in oversized jackets, with their funeral
pants at their ankles, top bananas with corn-
kernel teeth and tarantular breastbones; their colors,
paraffin, gesso, parched brain-coral, adobe; their
attitudes: prudery, venery, impenitence;
their posture, forensic; fingers
folded under, like the wingbones of bats, da Vinci
flying machines; a spider's remainder of hair; the
pupils discernible under their oval cocoons;
their sex, a fold in a pastry, slingshots, rosettes; some
raised to toe-point, sinews locking like
cloves into garlic, baroque or balletic, others
driving the total weight of their dying into their sandals;
ossobucco and tin in the shanks; rib cages
like empty prosceniums, burnt estuaries, smashed cradles—
children of cheesecloth and candles, Noh-devils
fetal again in their death-chambers of iron and chalk.

None will be naked again.

                    The covert
and promiscuous life of the newly unburied, the
flamboyance their breathing concealed or their body's
avidity made poignant and virginal—fountains of
semen and spittle, penetrations, erections—we know
now, were a gift of the spirit, expenses of grace and election.
Robbed of their nakedness, the dead are robbed of their mystery.
In their bellies' overturned sacks a feral pornographer
fingers a testicle, nipples and wombs turn
sterile: chewed-paper wasp nests, winter apples, prunes.

Yet it is in their mouths that they speak to us still. The shock
of encounter with—what? a collapse of the will? the preposterous?

nothingness? the terminal truths of betrayal?—
has opened their jawbones like grackles, sprung all the hinges,
turned all the lips heart-shaped: wolf-whistles, the coloratura's
invisible shout that splinters the wineglass, the leer
of a gargoyle's bravura.

                    Inside the cage there is screaming.

The buried, the gassed, the self-murdered, the
pregnant, burn in the ovens of Auschwitz, kindle and crackle
like napalm in a blind conflagration of noises
pitched out of range like the ears of a pointing retriever:
crying havoc, vendetta, universal rejection, universal derision,
the rage of the charlatan saint and the faulted believer.

We come out into sunlight, at last.
                        We see cut watermelons,
papaya, pyramidal oranges, gelatinous diamonds
where the pineapple sweetens its center in the hive's core.
We are wracked with the pangs of our fasting.
                            We are alive.
The children approach us with sugary ribbons:
"A mummy, señor?" And they offer us candy.

Mocking, solicitous, the children insist. The children wait to be paid.

We bite through the skulls in the cellophane wrappers.

We burn in the sunlight, afraid.

An Orange in Mérida

The orange-peelers of Mérida, in the wrought-
iron midday, come with mechanical skewers
and live oranges, to straddle the paths
on caissons of bicycle wheels
and work in the dark of the plaza, like jewelers' cloths.

The orange is ceremonious. Its sleep
is Egyptian. Its golden umbilicus
waits in pyramidal light, swath over swath, outwitting
the Caesars. It cannot be ravaged by knives,
but clasps its mortality in, like the skein of an asp.

The bandstand glitters like bone, in laurel
and spittle. Behind their triangular
catafalques, the orange-peelers move through the thirst
of the world with Rameses' bounty
caulked into the hive of the peel

while ratchets and wheels spin a blazing
cosmology on their little machines. Under
skewers and handles, the orange's skin
is pierced, the orange, in chain mail and papyrus,
unwinds the graveclothes of Pharaoh

in a helix of ribbon, unflawed, from the navel's
knot to the rind and the pulp underneath, like a butterfly's
chrysalis. And sleeper by sleeper, the living turn with their thirst
to each other, the orange's pith is broken
in a blind effervescence that perfumes the palate and burns

to the tooth's bite.
          And the dead reawaken.

From the Firehouse

(for Paul Feeley)

1. From the Firehouse

Living between two fires and two falls—a stairway
of watery risers and treads above and below, holding
the fish to its floor and the foam to the swallow's
intaglio, an Old Firehouse and a new—I think only
of canvas, like a Bedouin. Now in the whimsical
playground of your cellar, that birthday-box of aerial toys,
beginning with the color red, as children do,
I listen for engines folding their ladders in a burst
of exploding bells, a village in its underdrawers
wakened by the color red from its dream of sexual famine:
colors that bound from the canvas like a rubber ball
in a rite of counted jack-rocks, Cyclopean maces, panels
and chess pawns—your Euclidean signature, Paul.

And all night hear a skip-rope slapping canvas
between the crated sculpture and the mildewing gravel
where your boxer-father dances, shedding the color red,
lashing a corner of the Engine Room with his dream of travel
that flings you toward the Spanish littoral and flings
you back, shedding the color red, mortal Moroccan red.

I build a house as you would build in cards or canvas
with a gambler's riffle of whiskey and aces in spades,
or as your Damascan namesake built with a tent of
flames and sizing dazzled with lights and voices,
thumb to the palette like a bowling ball, breaking a string
of shapes and reassembling the shapes in identical frames
to demolish the spaces.

          Trout-hunter, dawdling in feathers
and flies, land-sailor skewed to an Irish passion for magnified
miniatures, miniature magnitudes—alternative symmetries
of the old wood-worshipers building with megaliths or
lacing the finical borders of the Book of Kells—bending your forms

The Old Firehouse, just across the street from the new, on Paran Creek in North Bennington, Vermont, served as studio for Paul Terence Feeley, the gifted American painter, until his untimely death in 1965, when it was converted into a storehouse for his canvases and a residence for his wife; and, more recently, a sublet for friends. —BB

with the precarious delineation of metal hammered thin and painting
the absences: fastidious illuminator: the shipwreck
on the Firehouse floor is not for you, beached for the night
like a clipper under gauzes and tarpaulins and butcher's papers.
I cannot bear the striking of your colors, that Sargasso of
passionate forms.

But sometimes from your sundeck I have seen
a crazy armada, canvas over canvas, break a storm
of sails, climb the stair to the millrace and the esplanade
of barns, burn with Egyptian extravagance in the maples
and window-glass, tacking toward Cydnus to call you from the dead
and paint our northern autumn with Pompeian red.

2. *Cat's Cradle*

Something the cat watches from his
cradle, in Ishmael's image,
his ear laid lightly
in swatches of crosshairs, like a
marksman sighting
a target of silence, the circuits
of a stethoscope's medallion,
looks back at the cat in midsummer
lightning and waits at a hole in the dark.

Something cavernous, cloacal, rank,
like a breathing of grills in a sewer
or a failed
stem in a glass
that thickened into mucus and then
stank; the frog on the well's floor, winy
with compost, ringed with ovulation;
the sac in the prawn's side, gorged;
the leaven in the whale's lump and the slime.

Dilating or sheathing his claws,
whiskered and spiked
like a Hapsburg, paws to his
ruff, with his eye-hairs
hiked in a vector, paring time
with his eye-slits,
the cat, from his crow's nest

on the creek bank,
predatory, tactical, binocular,

genius of speculation, feels
for a cause in the dark—
slippage of glaciers
and Pre-Cambrian corings, a
sleepwalking pigeon
shifting his stance or his feathers,
the mouse's tooth in a platen
of marrow, jeweled
on a hairspring of leather: feels

with the whole of his instinct,
dinosaur and serpent diminishing
to a purr—the whole
encompassment of darkness, invisible
ripenings like the bloom
on the underside of a leaf, darkness's
mother wit rising and falling, the bough's subtle
breathing where noon is the thickest—whether to
magnify being or make our nullity rich:

the cat will tell you which.

(for Jack Moore)

3. A Suicide: Paran Creek

> *"Give me my Robe, put on my Crowne, I have*
> *Immortall longings in me."*
>
> —Cleopatra

1.
The granny glasses under
their blind earpieces
folded over, the untimely cobalt
coat, quartered
into itself, and the painful
cane in the starved
March grass—put by
in decorous self-murder—

everything seemed urgent—

41

even the scum on the creek bank
where the millrace
smoked under flotsam
smelling of horsepiss, sour lumber,
detergent—

as, punctual to a fault,
you stayed to look your last
at the ordered streetlight, cropped
like a crozier, the Firehouse clock
in the car-barn
with its cunning pageantry of hoses,
its ambulance in yogurt and enamel
that might suddenly shriek,
whirl in a carousel—bells or
blood roses—

and with no hope
of manageable disaster—

you leaned to a muddy bottom,
all your length, face
down, as you would read
a hieroglyph of cancer and arthritis
and acedia, and left a floating answer
in the morning.

2.

(Yet something warmed you strangely
for a moment—a midsummer trick of swallows
over water, the trout's
whiplash under a shaking rainbow,
a black cat on the newspapers
and comics where a child
bought licorice strings—

or the "immortall longings"
of a sister who wore
Seleucid's stolen
bangles under her pharaoh's robe,
flinched in contrary cold: *"Your
crown's awry; I'll mend it
and then play . . ."*)

while you, her diffident neighbor,
alike in longing,
faced the other way at one
or two in the morning, hard-
hearted, anachronistic,
put off your steaming glasses
in Alexandrian blood-heat,
the blue, unseasonable coat, and
the cane beside them—just
as your note foretold—
and were delivered down.

4. *The Double-Goer: North Bennington*

1.
Seeing that dangerous mover,
we remembered the hazards of walking again:
the mastodon's trick
of stacking his spine on its child's box of blocks;
the mantis's walking-stick;
or the equilibrist
bearing down with the webs and the soles of his feet.
claw over crystal, and printing a town with his fists,
isometric, saurian, prehensile,
moving toward plunder.

2.
Face to face
with that obdurate profile pointed one way only,
drawn to its length like a bowstring,
with the noose
of a tie underneath, and a hatband
to level his jaw to the set of his teeth,
an arrowhead flinty with mourning,
insomniac, lonely—
coming or going we averted our glance when we met
and offered our backs to our guilt.

God help our uneasy walkers, we said. God hold
their weight to the invisible wheel
of their feet driving their anguish uphill

in all weathers; tether
their toes to the chains
moving over and under, tighten
the tendons and ratchets.
God true their purchase,
walking past taverns and graveyards in a hemorrhage
of leaves or the herringbone blue
of the snow. God make their placelessness perfect, going
nowhere, wherever they go.

3.
Where should a man walk in his fear and his need?
The gymnopede
walks out of his innocence into his vertigo,
rises and falls on his toes,
knowing all distance is mortal, all walking
demonic. The wanderer, trying his exile over and over,
measures his failing humanity,
and the stalker intending him harm
circles the sufferer, crumbles a spoor with his fingers,
and walks toward the print of his prey.

Only the walker keeps earthen.

The saltimbanque,
tumbling toward God, falls another way. The swimmer
working in fathoms, the breaker of ether,
alter their stance to their element
and forsake the old Adam. What was vertical,
durative, perishing,
falls like a diver or floats on a stilled horizontal.

Only the walker totters past the rattles and mats
of his childhood, erect, toward the sexual flaw
of his symmetry, goes frontal,
and doubles his burden.

4.
Even pity is helpless. Should we question
the bartering God—supposing
all action were fable, all
being, beginning: a "Prologue in Heaven"

or a charade for two players
bent over their pawns,
the unmoved movers of a dice-cup shaken by good and evil:
should we ask, midway in the walk:

"Why go looking for trouble? Why
lengthen your distance to hate us? Where do you walk?
Where are you from?"
—the answer already is given,
Belial's or Baudelaire's: *"From*
going to and fro in the earth and from walking up and down
in it. I am your Adversary,
homicidal or prodigal, Dutchman
or equivocal Jew, practicing life. I am Ishmael—
your brother, your double, your Other."

Solitudes

(Homage to Antonio Machado)

1. *Fat Tuesday*

Yesterday's
seven-thirty still clots the bandstand
clock. A child sleeps near the tinsel and papier-mâché
in a kerosene ring under the wavering flies.
The lovers embrace on the grandstand

as slowly
the machinery of celebration engages
its spokes and wheels around the incandescent center
of their pleasure. The plazas sparkle like stages
with a blind bicarbonation, and the masquers enter.

How simply
their dangerous reversal
is accomplished, the permutations of concealment
turning the cheesecloth and the mica of their disguises
into the dramatis personae of a dress rehearsal

and showing
the eye-hole's razor edges framing the double ovals
of the masquer's eyes, like buckets re-arising in a well, glowing
with vagrant spontaneities, the amateur's surprises
caught in the act of his improvisations.

Knowing
those Tuesdays of the flesh, reptilian
in their hungers, Antonio Machado, dragging his horsehair
greatcoat, his *Irregular Verbs for French Beginners,* the chalky
bastinado of his calling,

through the parched
Castilian school-day, in earshot of a parish's explosion,
scribbled a maxim in his *Marginalia:*
"Not to put on one's mask, but to put off one's face: that
is Carnival. The face alone in the world—that is appalling!"

And watched
from a cindery tussock how the masquers circled
a fountain in Baeza, putting off his cheekbones, eyes, the sensuous

underlip, emptying his skull of what it held
under the make-believe regalia,

leaving only
the arm-band of the widower's long deprival,
the schoolteacher who had "studied under Bedier and Bergson"
counting martlets between the bell-tower and horizon,
intent on the apocryphal and lonely.

And noted:
"The poet is a fisher in time: not of fish
in the sea, but the whole living catch; let us be clear about that!"
He put off his face, facing away from Madrid. The Tuesday of
    the guns grew fat.
He crossed the border into France, put on his mask and died into his wish.

2. *Boiling the Egg*

> *"Poetry is the word in its time; and students of poetry must maximize the*
> *temporality of their verse . . . All our class exercises have been devoted to*
> *this end . . . I especially remember a poem called* Boiling the Egg.*"*
>   —Juan de Mairena

On that morning of his exile
there was a sound of gunshot and zarzuelas from a nondescript
cantina. He looked toward Soria and Segovia, comedian
of the grieving countenance, packed his bag for France, and scoured his
    table-top
like an apothecary

to boil an egg. All
was in readiness: the mourners and personae of a lifetime—Meneses
and Mairena and Martín—the pestle and the mortar
of a broken boyhood, his widower's thirst, with its bucket on a ratchet
by the well, and a wheel

to draw his dearth up
from the cypresses and solitude of Castile—and, for his last vagary,
the battered barber's basin of a hero, sand from the Caves of Montesinos
to measure off the minutes of his hourglass; and the egg
shaped like a zero.

He lighted his spirit lamp,
candled his whimsical egg, as for some feat of prestidigitation,
turned back his watch-dial's fatal circuit to cancel out

47

the day, climbed the college ramp to erase a pedant's quibble—
     "*Dasein* into *Néant* into *Nada*—"
and began his peroration:

"That we must wait until the egg
boils or the door opens or the cucumber ripens is
something that merits your reflection, gentlemen!" The listeners
     drew closer.
"Democritus moves the atoms in the Universal Egg. But the boiling of
     the water
is the work of Heraclitus. It is

irreversible." And yet, how easily the boy
from Chipiona might have sucked that egg, blown out its white and yolk
through a pinhole in the shell, filled the void with perfume or confetti,
circled the circling lovers in the six-o'clock *paseo,* and smashed
the oval on a darkening carnival!

The egg boiled on, with none to see
the bloodlines in a map of Europe hardening in albumen,
the yolk melt down the crown of Montezuma, the caciques
of Isabella drink the steam up like a mushroom, Hiroshima's tissue-paper
skies catch fire in the conflagration.

He waited till the needle
splintered the spindle in his hourglass and the lingering bubbles ran to froth.
Only the egg remained, unscathed and disimagined in the burning.
Then he pinched the bluing flame with a forefinger, dinted
     the egg's perfection,
and moved forth on his journey.

3. *Journey of Abel Martín*
          (after Antonio Machado)

1.
Circling the bell-tower,
the martlets, trailing, soar:
children are storming the air and crying at their wars.
Adept in his solitude, Martín, in a corner there.
Evening or twilight making, dust
and a squabble of voices, a child's vociferations—
fifty or twelve, however you make it, all's one.

48

O starveling spirit and prodigal of soul,
by the glowering bonfire's circle
where dead sticks crackle in a fiery air
and blazon a blind frontier,
showing its blackest cicatrices clear!

The living shall surely perish, as Abel said.
Ah, distance, distance! the star
that none may handle, yet lightens the way ahead:
shall any voyage prosper, lacking it?

Great eye that looks on distance—O lessening sail!
Heart indurate in absence,
bland herbs
and honeys of love, blessed in forgetfulness.
Lore of the mastering Zero, of the rounded
fruit's quintessence ripening for man's need,
gout that breaks in a dream, and fountainhead of shadow,
shadow of godhead under the stretched, dread hand!
Before it be Day, if day be given, indeed,
the all-beholding light that is not yet come to pass,
whelm what is vile in me, outcry and exhortation,
Lord of all essences, and drown me in Nothingness!

2.
And that angel, skilled
in his secret, went out to Martín in the pass.
He gave him the little he had—the pietist's
pittance, perhaps? or a sop for extortionists?
Perhaps. But Martín there in the cold
knew himself lonely, strove with his knowledge, reproved
the Omnipotent Knower Who had no eye for His child,
and all that night in unspeakable wilderness moved.

3.
And saw his equivocal Muse
erect by his bedstead, the fugitive
haunting his streets, the bereft
and impossible love and the lady forever beloved.
And called to her: Lady,
for the uncovering of that face, my passion

49

thought to live until morning,
though my heart's blood turn to suet.
Wisdom is given me now. You are other than I dreamt.
Yet would I bless you still
and gaze the more, however you walked at your will,
at my side, in cold contempt.
                          Death turned to smile
at Martín, but knew no way to do it.

4.

I lived, I drowsed, I dreamed—
Martín thought, while his pupils thickened—
and thereby conceived a man in a slumbering vigil
intent on his dream, beyond what is dreamt or imagined.
Yet, if a harder reckoning be wanting,
equal for dreamer and watcher alike, the same
for those who apportion the roads
and those who follow them, panting,
conception in perfect nullity is yours, in the end:
the shadow of your presence, a colossus,
divinity left gazing at us blinded.

5.

First anguish; then exhaustion,
the pangs of despairing assurance:
the unappeasable thirst no water may ever diminish,
wormwood of time made poisonous with durance.

That lyre stretched for his dying!
                          Abel made trial with his hand
of his emaciate body.
Beholder of all that exists, did His vision not see him there, lying!
O the sloth of it, bleeding oblivion!

Help me, Lord help me!

                          His life, from its beginnings,
the unchangeable fable of his being, hovered,
traced on the yielding wax.
Would he melt, with the coming of day, in the sun?
Abel lifted a hand

to the light
of the vehement morning reddening into summer
that burned on the balcony of his dimming habitation.
Blinded, he groped for the glimmer he had never discovered.
Then he raised to his lips,
grown icier now, unhurried, the immaculate glass
of purest dark—O purest darkness!—brimming.

Antonio Machado (1875–1939), Spain's greatest master of the "Generation of '98," lived out a widower's life of deprival as teacher of French in high schools at Baeza, Soria, and Segovia, and died in exile in France toward the close of the Spanish Civil War. Among his final works is a volume of "apocryphal poems" and a collection of prose "epigrams, maxims, memoranda, and memoirs" of an "apocryphal professor" in whose guises as Meneses, Mairena, and Martín he disclosed the erotic and philosophical preoccupations of a lifetime.

—BB

This Scribe, My Hand

"When this warm scribe, my hand, is in the grave."
—John Keats

1.

You are here
on the underside of the page,
writing in water,

anachronist,
showing your head
with its delicate fuses,

its fatal telemetry,
a moundful of triggers and gunpowder
like a field-mine,

your sixty-one inches
and your gem-cutter's fingers,
anonymous,

taking the weight
of a "roomful of people"
but making no mark,

pressing the page as I write,
while the traffic in Rome
demotic with engines and klaxons

circles the Pyramid of Cestius,
crosses a graveyard, and submerges
again like the fin of a shark.

2.

I write, in the posthumous way,
on the flat of a headstone
with a quarrier's ink, like yourself:

an anthologist's date and an asterisk,
a parenthetical mark in the gas
of the pyramid-builders,

an obelisk whirling with Vespas
in a poisonous motorcade.
I make your surgeon's incision for

solitude—one living hand, two
poets strangled in seawater and phlegm,
an incestuous

ego to reach for
the heart in the funeral ashes,
a deathbed with friends.

3.

Something murderous flows
from the page to my hand—
a silence that wars

with the letters, a fist
that closes on paper: a blow
with the straight edge of a razor

that falls with a madman's
monotony, or the adze
of a sleepwalking Sumerian

nicking the wet of the clay,
hacking a wedge in a tablet
in the blood and the mica,

till all glistens with language.
The criminal folds up his claspknife. The shutters
slam down on the streets. *Nobody listens.*

4.

Out of breath with the climb, and
tasting a hashish of blood,
what did he see on the brink

of the Piazza di Spagna? A hand
in the frame of a cithara
where beggars and sunbathers

clotted the levels like musical
signatures, a Wordsworthian
dream of "degree," "unimaginable

time" touched by an axe
blade—or a pram
on the Steps of Odessa

torn from the hands of
its mother, gathering speed for the
plunge and rocking its tires

in the rifling, like a gun barrel,
smashing its way through the Tsar's
executioners, to a scream at the bottom?

5.

A failed solitude . . . The bees
in the Protestant grass
speak of it delicately

in the sweat of a
Palatine summer, guiding my hand
through the braille of the letters.

Violet, bluet, or squill—
what was it I picked
under the epitaph, what

rose to my touch
in the thirst of the marble, a cup
from the well of your grave

in the noonday miasma,
a hieroglyph in the water, saying:
solitude, solitude, solitude:

you have it at last—your
solitude writing on water,
alone with its failure.

6.

You are there
on the underside of the page,
a blue flower in my Baedeker,

writing on water. I know it.
The paper pulls under my pen,
peaks into waves

running strongly into the horizon.
The emptiness hardens
with balustrades, risers, and levels,

a staircase of Roman
azaleas. I slip on the blood and the ink
toward the exigent bed

of a poet. All is precarious. A maniac
waits on the streets. Nobody listens. What
must I do? I am writing on water

blazing with failures, ascending,
descending among lovers and trippers.
You are pressing me hard

under the paper. At Santa Trinità dei Monti
the stairway parts like an
estuary, rises and falls like a fountain.

There is nothing to see but a death-mask, your
room in an island of risers and treads, oddly
gregarious, an invisible hand in the granite.

7.

The tidal salts drain on a living horizon,
leaving a glare on the blemishing
paper. The silence is mortal.
                              Nobody answers.

                    (for Joan Hutton Landis)

Block Island: After The Tempest

"Lie here, my art!"
                    —Prospero

1. *Block Island Crossing*
                    "What is't? A spirit?
                    It carries a brave form. But 'tis spirit."
                         —Miranda

Crossing at Point Judith, one feels the world's
doubleness in the walloping stance of the Ferry—
Elisha's marvelous flatiron afloat in the fog
like a prophet's token: the boat and its baggage,
its plucky machinery, its cautionary noises,
swampy or soft-spoken, dividing the watery
flannels without wrinkle or seam to their destination.

Below, inlanders, islanders. A stable
of station-wagons. The cold-drink and the hamburger
concession with its branding-iron's sizzle
of stabbed bicarbonation, mustard in tumblers
under a gable of bulbs.
                    Outside, the yielding opalescence
and the steam, the nearly visible folding and unfolding
of the spaces, fog in its thermal channels
scudding the levels with a gull's evasions,
flying its semaphore of noises, bell-
clappers, conch-sounds, to a clutter of island pilings.

For suddenly, it is *there!*

                    Somehow, in the drenched
displacement, a boat no bigger than a haddock
asserts its ungainly will to cross, with its gimcrack
universe intact, endures its self-effacement and its loss
and heaves a hawser to the opposite landing.

                         The Island
waits, placed and substantial. What was double or indistinct—
the rose-hip and the cranberry and the pure precipitation
that effaced them—merge in a common passion for existence.
Headlands and beaches, the Lighthouse in the middle
distance, open their burning vectors on the water,

with a map-maker's precision, circle the air
with soundings to say where the rock was ambiguous,
the ferry's bow and the Village, a single vision.

There is light on the bluffs and light enough in the berry.

We know what the dove knows in our casual
chaos.
        The gangway is down.
                        A mountain dries for us.

                        (for Mary Jo Shelley)

2. *Southeast Lighthouse*
                ". . . teach me how
        To name the bigger light, and how the less."
                        —Caliban

Chaos is always thère. The Lighthouse's gesture,
poised on its needle, sweeping a compass's foot
three hundred and sixty degrees in chalk and acetylene,
mapping, unmapping, sowing and scything the air,
erasing the seas, tells us in freezing graffiti:
the chaos is there, it is there!

Night shows us a blind man's cane—light, tapping the rocks
of an arranged interior whose dangerous threshold is fixed
in a salt parabola, so the keel may not utterly drown
in the doorway, the seven white and the eight black blocks
of the headland not suddenly reverse themselves, the watcher
hallucinate and go down,

as the furniture of ocean pitches us toward a window
where the slain eye looks at crazy tungsten raking
the zenith with its platinum track, Toledan or Damascene, raw
with the burin's filings—seeing nothing
yet mapping a lane in the brine where Oedipus or Lear
might walk as though they saw:

Saw the ship come unbroken to the pilings, as if
it had learned something of the plummet; saw the skeptical cities succumb
in the night of punishing water; saw chaos itself
at last, unmoved by the word of God, while the face

of the deep still looked out of darkness toward a negative
finger, and was dumb.

For nothing has been created. Nothing! Nothing! All is yet to come.
The cloud that whirls in the Lighthouse's vector confirms
the superstitious dream of Adam and the geography of danger,
the staggering keel in the shipwreck, the gull's wing bloodying glass.
The ocean spins emptily. The Lighthouse counts three hundred and sixty
     degrees. And the salt
comedy of unknowing begins.

3. *Soundings*

     "I'll drown my book!"
        —Prospero

1.
The sea closes like a plum
on its stone. It will presently fall.
Halfway toward Newton's head

it shows a nap of numbers,
rosettes for the navigator,
under the mariner's glass, a gooseflesh of soundings—

a flat map where gulls enter
reading the fine print in tawny aquarelle. Later,
that ripping of edges

at the Lighthouse's base, a pounding
of tumblers and bells in the coarse salt,
the reef in its necklace of skulls.

2.
Whales work. A swan, leading its cindery cygnets,
sees transparently down
to the center: Alice's tears, the nausea of Rimbaud,

green gall and spittle
to pucker the sea floor, constellate
polyps in the flinty asparagus,

the unsuffocating flora
where the diver's heart explodes
in crossthreads of mica and the sardine throbs like a hummingbird—

all the bright business of darkness
I would read in the charred scrolls, the double pillars
of vellum, crossing with chariots, like Torah.

3.
The parachutists lie where they have fallen
on mandalas of terry cloth. The sea has cast
them up like anemones, split prismatic canvas

in spinnakers of beach umbrellas. A sound
of drowned transistors, gulls' claws in the froth,
a lifeguard's whistle, the breathing of pontoons,

hisses through the noon's bicarbonation.
Light hardens the facets. But there, in the sleeper's
eye, the glacial emulsions of a camera,

sight keeps its core of darkness—
an apple, halved, and in the satin pockets, point
touching point, like Indian paisley, the seed-shaped tears.

4.
What holds the eye to its salt, Orphean
lookers-back, Sodomites, ruminants
licking a briny meniscus—

what? The pastures of plankton,
coffined nerve-gas, sarcophagi
lifted like thistle three miles under,

are not as inland meadows are. There,
green goes aerial, drives star over star through the chicory,
stays nowhere, asks nothing of the malcontent. But here?

Something unappeasable
in the blond marination of whips, melancholy
bearing night in its bile: an expectation of black.

5.
Failures! The thunderheads of bracken
rise over minefields, the sea burns
like a slum, sends arabesques of oil

on all my summer salvage:
young losses, nightmares, a kneecap smashed,
or a back, forfeiture of sons,

the wild severity of poems,
the mouth's sanctuary, the Mona Lisa smile
of adolescent bellies sloping toward their sex,

drowned fathers, photographs, translations
in the middle kingdom of the languages—
fog, foam, hallucinated form.

6.

Noah's drunken dream: the animals in twos,
delineated water, rainbows. Fog works in the mummy-cloths;
the sandspit goes, in its spiral nebulae of boulders,

the millrace of the upper air, flying
iodine, the binnacle's
mathematics, battlefields of bathers,

the Pharaonic sun that calcifies the beaches
and cuts the swimmer's diamond in the sand,
the light dividing water from the land,

matter, motion, mind—all goes to bandages,
equinoctial steam. The floating bobbins empty,
bearing the corpse of darkness toward the ocean.

7.

Block Island, Black Island*; Pablo, Prospero—
how utterly the landmarks tarnish!
Our "residence on earth" shows spiracles,

watery torches, shark's fins, the purgatorial jaw
of Jonah's disobedience. *It is time
for the breaking of wands and books.*

The rose-hip looses
its petal on the blackberry's dagger
under the certain apparition of a ship,

Isla Negra—"Black Island": the Pacific retreat of Pablo Neruda

and I enter the desolating soda
again, taking the whole weight of the sun upon my skin
to drive the darkness in.

(for Pablo Neruda)

4. *Freshwater Pond*
> *"Where the bee sucks, there suck I."*
> —Ariel

The parting of waters should make
a swarthier sound than this:
a noise like the breaking of bronzes
in alluvial silt, Rameses'
chariot wheels, the tambourines
of Deborah and Judith,
Armageddons, hosannahs—

but here where the wars of bayberry and peat
sweeten the whole of a promontory,
invisible hexagons meet
in a swarming of salts,
driving their honey and gall
throught the core of a continent's
fault, to hum like the wax of a hive.

The line of the spit where the
snapping turtle and monogamous swan
forage for sugar, glares in a jungle
of cattails. No one can say where
the salt of the juggernaut stalls,
or the bland and the bitter cross over
to mesh like the grids of a sieve.

Yet heavily, heavily one way the facets
of brine drop their plummet's weight
in vaults of acidulous bracken
to harden in iron and manganese;
and the other way the sweets in the rose-hip

climb up a thicket of seeds and leaven their wine
on the summit for Ariel's pleasure.

(for Virginia Carlin)

5. *A Choppy Sea*
> *"All corners else o' th' earth*
> *Let liberty make use of. Space enough*
> *Have I in such a prison."*
> —Ferdinand

The world's containment, provisional
as porcelain or crystal—a cup's
clasp on an abyss
or the upward look from a gorge
through a fillet of leaves at Andromeda riding the zenith,
Tiepolo's goddesses skewed on a dome's
umbilicus—persuade us we are finite and bring us at length
to an ocean balancing an island like an egg in a spoon.

Shelf over shelf, the continent offers its brim,
gathers in basins and columns,
a rising and falling of wells,
Corinthian water or the pillars of Angkor Vat. Spending
and replenishing itself, the void fills like a bucket,
the ocean creaks and goes taut,
a dipper empties, and the fountains of Genesis
soak their way through the cisterns and blacken the ledges.

The gull sees it with a predator's
excitement: confinement's opposite angel, overplus,
that lives on the thirst of the starved and abstemious.
Over the platter, the pitcher: the pit of the cataract,
windlass, the trough and the pail,
the underground spilth of a world that feeds on excess
and shows the way to the depths—
the granaries under the shale and the magnets
that sleep in the forms,
pulling continents, islands, messengers, into the eye of the storm.

But nothing will happen today.

A bather stands on a sandbar feeling the sinister
freeze at his ankles. A sailboat tightens its cloths.
High tide: with a tarry light in the greens.
A foaming of potsherds, anthracite flaking the spray,
Indian arrowheads.

Three forty-five. The ferry is punctual.
                                        The pylons yaw
and give way.

            It is a choppy sea.

6. *Nighttown: Block Island*
        *"Here's neither bush nor shrub to bear any weather at all, and
        another storm is brewing."*
                                        —Trinculo

Nothing will happen today. The clammers
are back from the sand-flats, with crystals of chitin
and silt in the slats of their buckets.

The yachts have gutted their catch in the Basin,
slashed filet and roe from the fishbones and construed
all the entrails. The haruspicies are good.

The lights go out at Ballard's and Baroni's. Trinculo
lies down in his litter of six-packs to dream of banquets and noises.
The adolescents pair off in the Lutheran curfew.

The streets stream toward an ocean mapped out with
nautical numbers. In the lattices of porches the Lighthouse's helix
hones its facade of Victorian scrimshaw and gingerbread—

all the banked transportation of bicycles,
boathouses, bell buoys, triangular flags to point
to the weather tomorrow, blind polaroid, sun lotions.

Only the headlands show garnets and blues,
a tunnel of melting graffiti fogged with initials
and gases—submarine, subterranean.

But something is pulling the pylons
askew in the underground cities, gnawing away the foundations.
The plumb lines that fasten the tides to the craters

and calculate deserts are tilting a continent's biases.
The oceans are drying to peat on their shelves, the peat into cinder
and flint. Chaos is showing its hearthbed of iron

again, black holes and barnacles, the fiery maws
of a starving leviathan. In the dark of the morning
a planet is turning to ether, as midwinter landscapes

efface themselves under snow. An island is going
to blubber and fin, a garbage for krakens, streamers
of pitchblende, coronas. There are warnings.

All hangs in the balance. All waits for the
rubbery boots of a sword-fisher, a deckhand to fold the drowned
tarpaulins and open a lane to Portugal.

Ariel comes with his tray for the drunkards
in a thicket of berries and cutlery. Big-bladdered, they stand
to the arch of their urine, caryatids supporting a rainbow; and

nothing will happen today.

III
Nowhere But Light
(1964–1969)

"There is nowhere but light."

The Orange Tree

To be
intact and unseen,
like the orange's scent
in the orange tree:

a pod of aroma
on the orange's ogive of green
or a phosphorus voice
in the storm of the forge and the hammer:

to climb up a ladder of leaven
and salt, and work in the lump
of the mass, upward and down
in the volatile oils of a wilderness heaven:

to sleep, like the karat,
in the void of the jeweler's glass,
yet strike with the weight of the diamond—
perhaps that is to live in the spirit!

So the orange tree
waits on its stump as the wood of its armature
multiplies: first, the branch, then the twig in the thicket
of leafage, then the sunburst of white in the leaves, the odor's epiphany.

All burns with a mineral
heat, all hones an invisible edge of the noonday, while the orange's scent
speaks from the tree in the tree to declare what the holocaust meant:
to be minimal,

minimal: to diminish excess; to pare it
as a child pares an orange, moving the knife through the peel
in a spiral's unbroken descent, till only the orange's sweat,
a bead of acidulous essence, divides the rind from the steel:

perhaps that is to live in the spirit.

Dog in the Manger

Thunder has driven us
where darkness interprets the animal—
under the shears and the picture frames,
the gardening gear in the cellar—
to a furnace in banded asbestos
ticking its waterdrop sounds,
mop-cords of hardening naphtha,
pulverized ram's-horn dung.

There, lives the crazed and unkillable
gift of her vigilance, the creaturely
fear that tightens the line of her jawbone,
while her fangs in their tortoise-shell
markings draw me into her skull
in a shine of bitumen
and we know ourselves frightened. We are stopped.
We look back toward the pillars

of garbage alive in the working aluminum,
storm-windows stacked, copper
and iron and oil, the gout of the gas
honing its tooth with a midsummer
midge's sound, to the troglodyte's world
that lies under the world of the human.
The house that she carries somewhere
on her back—a totem

of excrement, a shipwreck
of clapboards and shutters, an ark
that boils on the froth of the gutters—
rise and falls on its drains
while we watch for some presence
that troubled the waters. The darkness is heavy,
with a smell like a spade's wedge.
Our spittle is dry . . . We ride over the edges

together, and I call through the darkness:

Here, Daffy!

Here, Daffy!

Chipmunks

The sweet playfellow
is already aware.
Taking a safe-cracker's stance
and turning the tumblers of air,
his paunch set down
like a reticule,
his ballerina's eyes
sootily bowed back
as for *Swan Lake*,
dancing the word for surprise
with his henna behind
and the tungsten crook
of his tail, his ears
like an adze
in the cinnamon and black
of his face's triangulations.

What draws love to its object,
unlike to like, impure to pure,
as my eyes to this?
The chipmunk, balancing the spike
of the acorn on prayed paws,
knowing the stations of the rodent,
finds kernel and meat
with his nose,
like any other rat,
and packs the pulp home
with his jaws.
By wainscoting and sewer
a killer keeps his vigil
by a trap:

Love is content with that.

On Quaking Bog

(for Tom and Jean Brockway)

When the Walkers-on-Water went under,
the Bog-Walkers came out of the barberry
thickets, booted in gum to their hips,
in a corona of midges, their ears electric
with sound, beating the stale of the swamp
with their whips and flailing the ground
for the itch under the frond, the fern's
demonology, the mosquito's decibel.

Night-sweat clotted their palms. They tasted
their gall. The sumac flickered a swatch
of its leaves in the lichens and venoms,
a dazzle was seen in the fog
as a vegetal world gave way to a uterine,
pitch pulled at their heels and blackened
their knuckles, the bog-laurel's fan
opened its uttermost decimal and showed them the Bog.

Paradisal, beyond purpose or menace, dewed
like the flesh of an apple with the damp
of creation, the disk of the pond glowed
under the dragonfly's bosses, where a faulting
of glaciers had left it—vaults of bog-rosemary,
buckbean and Labrador tea, a dapple
of leavening mosses soaking in ice water, peat-wicks
feeding their gas to the cranberry braziers.

They entered the bonfire together. The moss
took their weight like a trampoline:
they walked on the sponge and bitumen without
leaving a footprint. In between,
in the vats of mat-roses where the waterline
closed like a skin, the ambiguous
world of imbalance, non-being, the pre-human
and tentative, was one with the ludicrous.

The quaking began—under their bootsoles
at first, like a whale under ambergris,
then cramming their wrists with a drummer's
vibrations, knocking their ribs and their knees

as all sagged and rebounded. They lurched on the wet
as though tracing a profile of breakers
or displacing the cords and the voids of a net,
and staggered back into their childhoods,

till their feet touched the granite again.
The Bog tossed them back, and the threshold
opened a path in the spruce toward the opposite
edges. The leaves closed behind them. They walked
an unyielding and tangible world like strangers, remembering
only the hovering glare where the pitcher-plant's
hammer closed on the fly—the light shaking and shaking—
as a pulse touched their feet from below, and passed over.

Salto de San Anton

(Saint Anthony's Falls)

We are summoned, we know,
by no great thing—a sound's
excitement, the panache of the spray
on the quill of the waterfall—
to witness some self-expense:
a break in the river's bed
that opens the stone and makes it aerial.

We wait on the cavern's anvil,
not knowing yet
whether to complete or contain or demolish
the thing we contemplate,
feeling addition and loss, the abyss's overplus,
the hammers of gossamer pounding the feathery glosses
while the stones take a thornier polish—

and the thing we would re-create, the withheld
and the given thing,
conclusive, apocalyptical—
the column of force aloft on the basin's edge
and the bow in the column—
fails in a sickle of water, a glow on the flat of a precipice
like light under a threshold
where the insomniac questioner, turning the pages of water,
the troglodyte under the Gorge,
feels the bottomless cold of the source,
the burning away of the brim.

The Gorge

(Cuernavaca)

1. *View from the Gorge*

Doré knew this overhang.

                          He cut
his cortège for the damned on those levels
to carom on the magnets and springs in the banging
of gongs and the lights of his pinball *commedia.*

In his black-and-white
world, the ascents and descents of the Gorge,
the roots, like a fistful of entrails, the hachure
of pitchblende and acid that abuts
on that ordered logistics for sinners,
lead to a fall or a forge.
                         The odds
are already well known: electric displays for the winners,
and the damned circling down toward the hammers.

What holds me today
is the purgatorial moment, seen small on the opposite side,
on the tilt of the slope where the gardeners
move in the marzipan whiteness, squared off
like a waffle. Quicklime
has dazzled the glass of the greenhouses there,
sugared the ovens of Hansel and Gretel
where a work of redemption begins
in the alternate lines of the cuttings—bougainvillaea
and palm on the ledges—blazing giddily in buckets and tins.

Some loving solicitude has motioned the mannikins there
to hover like dragonflies and settle like seeds in the air—
to balance all day
on a long foot, for purchase, with the shorter
doubled into their shoulders—penitential, half mantis,
half angel, on a causeway of manna and boulders.

And the moment suffices.

What lies plane at the top
like a sponge-rubber glaze for an architect's table

or a primitive ceiling;
what we guess from below in the clot of the mangroves:
the generations of Rahab, the fires and the basalt of Dante, the bones
of the beast of Apocalypse, Quetzalcóatl
and Grendel in the offal and trash of our sins—

these were an earlier fable.

In between go the gardeners, with the grace of the hummingbird's
balance, who bend to the slope
in the quicklime and flowers, planting knowns
and unknowns, because sun shines exceedingly there
and the spirit is willing.

2. *The Loco-Bird*

The loco-bird flies over the Gorge,
tilts on a scrub-palm, at his metaphysical
angle, looks down from his glinting
propellers, and takes in his prize, at a glance.

          All my awe
at the slant and equivocal—all
I have stood on its head in behalf of the wonder
that sharpens the bat's wit and tightens his decibels
to portents and sounds from down under,
is undone by his stance.
       Whatever Zochipili heard
in the flint and the scoriae, the loco-bird sees
what is there to be seen:
two quicksilver drops on the cusp of a fern, and a turd.

Back in the tulipan, he rattles his beads
and enamels. Moving out of the down-drafts unawed
by obliquity, all's one to him: a
descent in a maelstrom or a herringbone
climb up a Matterhorn—the loco-bird swivels
his rudders, steadies his keel, and skates off,
chaplinesque,
on a rink, in the steerage, a spa, an alarm clock,
a lady's emporium, a steam-bath with the peerage:
he knows how its feels
to look into the billy and badge of the actual

74

and veer out of range on his wheels
without ruffling his daily sensorium.

He fills the whole tree with his presence.
His tail-feathers take on the expansive designs
that our grandmothers mounted in isinglass: India ink
on a background of spirals and pampas-grass, absurd in the litter
of florid calligraphy. He blackens the leaves
with the crow's iridescence,
while a sound issues forth from the glitter:
not madness, not the anger
of Timon or Lear on the heath, but the gratified scream of the bird
of the abjectly ridiculous—a sound like a child's smutty fingertip
rubbing the damp of a shaving-glass; or a glasscutter's wheel
over glass; whistles and burps; an acetylene blast;
and the banging of a safe-cracker's tools in an empty museum.

All tumbles into the Gorge.
bounces off into nothing from level to level, is absorbed in the stream.

It says: *The devil walks to and fro in the world, the devil . . .*

But the bird in the tulipan tree has no answers.

3. *"Gayosso" Ambulance Service: Emergency*
        (Cuernavaca to Mexico City)

Feet-last,
on Gayosso's tea-caddy for corpses
and convalescents, all seemed an
"emergency." Already
the colors had charred in the tulip-trees,
batons and vibrations
barred on a cereal zodiac, while I rolled
underneath toward the van
in my onion of blankets.

The idea of nonbeing,
the broths and syringes, cocoons
of miraculous molds and detergents that spoke
of a "turn for the worse," swirled
in the headlights. The gorges turned backwards,
the city sloped under my shoulders in a rocket-burst

starring the Valley of Mexico. All tripped like a lens and a shutter
on the flare of a moment and spoke for the traveler:

"Urgent!"

Urgent?
          And what of the fraud of that "safety"?
The clown climbing the clock in the celluloid,
the tortoise-shelled
yokel brilliant with nausea, caught
on the clock-face, on the pin and the pointer, riding
his belt-buckle, knows better. . . .
                         One walks as one can
on the vertical planes
of the windows like ties on a trestle,
looking fifty flights down to a dumb-show of
Stock-Exchange runners; one slips
toward the tooth of the buzz-saw
while the freight-cars bear downward from Toonerville,
sparkling with danger.

So the scene recomposes itself,
undemure in its aftermath, "drawn to scale."

Having rented a cut in the Gorge
in a weather where even the tiles on the facing embankment
are plain, one endures the precarious.
                    Always,
crossing the tulipans, somewhere—
Gayosso's "emergency" rides on the scream
of a moment: the lateral life of the "urgent"
centers and sways on an ego, like a carpenter's bubble;
the equilibrist falters,
shocked by his personal hazard.

                    But another sound
lives in the Gorge—
an equivocal threshing of bamboo and manure and papyrus,
neither pure nor impure: the spirit
that works in the middle,
stark under the sun-stone,
in the mash of the upper and nether.

And, heard as the Gorge-Dweller

hears it, the serpent's tail beating the shell,
that unriddles its birth in the wet and the dark

and says: *It is well.*

It is well.

4. *Full Moon: The Gorge*

With the moon at full, its blind side
falls toward the Gorge: two flintstones kindling
a glare in sidereal trash: tin-tops, bottles, and glasses
starring the foliage with the constellation of The Pair—
a pubis of blackening mangrove on a pubis of ash,
a mating of firmaments, fatal and beautiful, there.

All absent things move toward their fullness now:
all shaping artifacts, essences, human similitudes,
briny or bloody deluges, sweat-drops, semen, and air,
all troubled tossings of parturitive foam
or fiery paradigms that work in the perishing
flesh to dazzle the pulses and sparkle like mustard seeds
for the bird in the animal excrement, the ammoniac singer—

toward that zenith warmed by the sunlight, the egg in the down
of exorbitant dark: light's underside,
where the pottering flyer fails on Canaveral
and, one after one, the universes disclose themselves
in the gravitational swamps, as noonday burns to its socket

and is night. Night. Night as I would have it,
night that I sought in its festival guises as sun-stone,
planetary rose, salt with its faceted enigmas, fern,
fires of the sexual whale saying: *I am! I made it!* in
catastrophic sperm, love's underside, love's failings, tears—

yes, love's ignominious reversals that my heart's starvation
would have reversed, if it could: night with its names for powers,
dominations, fears: houses, Homeric fictions: Dante astray
in the tiger-taken wood: Hell with its vortical vengeances:
and night, night without respite or guile, the light of common day.

Cutting the Bittersweet

The quarrelers in bittersweet,
saviors and butchers, too late for stealth,
are here in the August morning, in the first of the heat,
with their stilted pruning shears and their puritan hate

to root out the trespasser, berry and branch,
in a country vendetta. They have seen
how the strangler advances with trident and net,
forcing its pod in the thicket of lilac—

the gratuitous killer whose
grievance is everywhere, scribbling the margins
with threats, cutting anonymous letters
in the broadening leaf: who stabs through the stake and the splint

to gather a mangled typography
and extort the whole plenty of summer: the crime
that shows only the glint of its appetite, the red of the bittersweet
berry, to say what catastrophe means

and speak for the mindless destroyer. But justice
is manifest. A pruning-fork works
in the cluster. The noose of the bittersweet opens
its spirals and layers, disengaging

the rose and the poplar, and surrenders its murderous
sign: a cutting of ovals and staves,
like a musical signature, a bonfire alive on the stones.
And the searchers in bittersweet—those whom the summer

left nothing, the red-handed ones bereft in a winter
of holly: the parasitical borrowers,
time-servers, counterfeiters, the clingers and latecomers,
gather the harvest indoors.

(for Anne Schlabach)

Winter Pond: Lake Paran

(for Jo Van Fleet)

Lest the ripple deceive us
with its midsummer dazzle, a cat's-paw
of lustre on the shimmering weight of the water,
and the Heraclitean swimmer
dissolve into light, scarring the pond
with his passing—arm over arm in the herringbone ringed with a gas—
and no one believe us:

I stand in the March
of my mind in a winter perspective:
suds, scurf, cobble—a sherbet of blackening ice
with a pylon inset on a lunar enormity, and beyond
it, a tractor in characterless orange:

the lake like an adamant
drawing into the flint and the salt
all a planet's mobility—algae and perch,
the gelatinous hives of the frog, night crawlers,
the semen and freeze of a winter—until
all locks, like a cluster of crystal,
lifts up in its basin in its perfect containment,
a monolith crowding the shale,
a troglodyte's hammer
pounding the weathers and pressing on obdurate matter
like the light on the pomegranate's rind,
or the bones and the scales of a carp.

The seasons disclaim us. But a shock lives on in the air—
a pulse like a forge in a cloud
that beats on the latent and makes the ambiguous bearable.
Facet by facet, we assemble a vanished relation—
the swimmer under the ice and the skater on water—
harden the edge of our world till our images name us
and the possible touches the heart and declares what it saw:

an ice-floe that burned in the thaw,
the hailstone's precipitation
that opened a well for the noon of the fish and the flycaster,
set a bow on the ripple, recovered the spinner's vibration,
till all was motion and passion and presence, flashing as never before:

And the swimmer arose in his nakedness and called from the opposite shore.

Papermill Graveyard

(North Bennington, Vermont)

In that country of thresholds we move like vandals
overturning birth dates, death dates, necrologies, Bartlett's
Familiar Quotations, the exorbitant rhetoric
of compliment, spelling hard names, looking for pictures
under the blackboards of a child's stone library
of aphorisms. In the runt gardens and the greenhouse
"arrangements"—pinwheels of laurel in plastic, jelly-jars
crammed with wildflowers not meant to outlast
an homage, the rancid memoranda of the very poor—
all is remembered. Each gives to each in a ghastly
plenty: the intimacy of a terminal cough
recalled in formaldehyde and licorice, a bull's-eye of death trance,
the husband's abandoned spasm in a barrow of granite,
endearments, betrayals. The tribal successions of the unexceptional man
are plausible here. Even the destitute scribble their heraldries.
The soldier schooled in a captive security, mistrusting the living,
salutes the interrogator with name, rank, and serial number.
Under the chintzy flags, holidays, holocausts, individual
deaths, the unlucky recruit, blinded by chevrons, is caught
in the scintillation of family keepsakes, a rabbit's foot
crossing the spaces in search of savory greens. All
remains minimal: footlockers of Government Issue
cut frugally to size, berry-boxes for the stillborn,
mortuary cabinets indexed under Urgent Business
in an Erechtheum of furnished pillars
where death begets death and nothing comes of nothing.

Having nothing to memorize but an expatriate spirit,
her chemist-husband, married, unmarried, remarried, the epithalamial
rasp of a cello-string and the kindness of friends who covered her loss
with a willow, I forage for trifles—the maggot's hammer-blow,
a lawn-mower's blade in the chicory, my face on the bevel
of granite glazed over *"Mother"* and *"Father."*

But this is no trifle.
Jeanne Butler, Jeanne Butler, Jeanne Butler—how strangely you lean

toward the heel of my hand, still living on your nerves, severe in your Breton
cheekbones, repeating the uvular *r* for schoolgirls from Cambridge, settling
your napery while our teacups bitter in a garden
over pitted persimmons broken and eaten together, and a changing wind
works in the wafer's paste, hardens the knife's edge, and delivers
our unhaunted world to the Prince of Darkness!

Veterans' Hospital

(White River Junction, Vt.)

Bringing "only what is needed—essential
toilet articles" in a paper bag,
dressed as for dying, one sees the dying plainly.
These are the homecomings of Agamemnon,
the odysseys to the underside of the web
that weaves and unweaves while the suitors gorge upon plenty
and the languishing sons at home unwish their warring
fathers, with strong electric fingers.

                    The fathers are failing.

In the Hospital Exchange, one sees the dying plainly:
color televisions, beach towels, automatic razors—
the hardware of the affluent society marked
down to cost, to match the negative afflatus
of the ailing, the bandages and badges of their status.
Under the sandbags, rubber hoses, pipettes, bed-clamps—
tax-exempt, amenable as rabbits,
the unenlisted men are bleeding through their noses
in a perimeter of ramps and apparatus.

In that prosthetic world, the Solarium
lights up a junkpile of used parts: the hip that caught
a ricochet of shrapnel; tattoos in curing meats;
scars like fizzled fuses, cancelled postage stamps;
automated claws in candy; the Laser's edge; and barium.
The nurses pass like mowers, dressing and
undressing in the razor-sharp incisions
and the flowering phosphorescence. The smell
of rubbing alcohol rises on desertions and deprivals
and divorces. It is incorruptible. A wheelchair aims
its hospital pajamas like a gun-emplacement.

The amputee is swinging in his aviary.
His fingers walk the bird-bars.

                    There is singing
from the ward room—a buzzing of transistors
like blueflies in a urinal. War over war,
the expendables of Metz and Château Thierry,

the guerrillas of Bien Hoa and Korea,
the draftees, the Reserves, the re-enlisters,
open a common wavelength.
                          The catatonic
sons are revving up their combos in the era
of the angry adolescent. Their cry is electronic.
Their thumbs are armed with picks. The acid-rock guitarist
in metal studs and chevrons, bombed with magnesium,
mourns like a country yokel, and the innocents
are slaughtered.

                On the terrace, there are juices
and bananas. The convalescent listens to his
heartbeat. The chaplain and his non-combative daughter
smile by the clubbed plants on the portico.

                                        "They shall overcome."

1966: The Stonemason's Funeral

"Shaftsbury Stone Mason and Son Die Under Wheels of Vt. Railway Train While Hunting"
—Headline, *Bennington Banner* (Vt.), November 23, 1966.

1.

"Are you there, son?"
          "Here. All here!"

I think of the wheels: what the wheels meant:

the cement-mixer by the walled garden,
its conical jet's nose
kneading quicklime, semen, cement,
tilted and turning . . .

and the half-naked ones
seen from above—the son, the father, the son—
filling the troughs of cement
at the great wall's center, in the stonemason's way:
the stone rose, the stone heart of the artichoke,
the marrow and block of the burning—

or drinking cold Cokes in the cavernous lilac,
the sun on their nipples, their nostrils, their sex,

on their backs, and at rest.

2.

I think of the hunt: what the father was hunting—

paring boulders to bone,
angling and shunting the edges
of granite, fitting facets like pineapple-rinds, forcing rubble
and shell like flint for an arrowhead—

what was he hunting there, with the hod on his shoulders
and the brick and the straw of the Hebrews behind him,
the Great Wall of China, the tower, the well,
the winnowing wheels and the millstones of Gaza,
the tables of bran and macadam—

What would strike through the granite, to find him?

3.

I think of the wall: what the stones meant:

the son, the father, the son,
piling their burial barrow in the nightshade and lilac,
in the cold sweat of Adam:

What blackened the boulders with the horn
of the Scyldings,
circled the rooftops
of Stonehenge, the quarries of Syracuse,
the megaliths
pointing their profiles toward Easter Island
like the dial of a petrified garden:

what were they building
to make an unbreakable world in the dews of the terrace?

4.

"Are you there, son?"
                    "Here. All here!"

                              "Keep
your flashes down low. Feel for the brush with your toes.
Drop onto your heels and set them down light.
No use to startle the deer in the dark!"

                              "Right!"

"Watch for the horns of the buck. Stand clear
of the does. We'll double on back
where the path takes the turn by the overhang
and crosses the railroad track.

                    "Good luck!"

5.

I think of the wheel: what the wheels meant:

the barred boxcars, the freights passing over
a seamed span of track like a carpenter's
rule opened flat to its length
in the gravel and thistle—

cowcatcher, lanterns, and cistern, the rust of the trestle,
the switch—

then a spindle of light like a burning-
glass focused on nothing, frosting the clover like glass,
the acidulous smell of the sand on the spikes and the steel
of the crossties—the whistle . . .

till the ruby that held the caboose to its track
spiraled into the jewel of a railroader's watch
and clicked shut—

and the journey was over.

6.

I think of their deaths: what their deaths meant:

having set the last boulder
with the stonemason's cunning that steadies the block
from within, in the pith
of cement, showing only the coarse outer edges, and the spaces
dividing the stones, held in precarious balance
like a zodiac circling a sun—

the son, the father, the son,
pursuing the deer
over crossties of mica like stepping-stones cut for the path
of the steam's effervescence, the whistle, the wheel, and the scream—

having come to the place they had sought: the underground
door in the green of the terraces,
the mastodon's mound in the nightshade and bittersweet:
having said:

> "We have seen antler and horn in the labyrinth."

They sealed the great threshold, set the altar-stone over the plinth,
signed the mortar and bricks
with a wreath of initals and three copper pennies

dated: *one nine six six.*

Moon Walk

It is time to re-invent life,
we say, smelling ammonia from Mars
in a photograph, seeing right angles
in galactic soda, a glass bead from a crater,
the color purple.

        To that enormous death's head
we bring the constellation of Snoopy and Charlie Brown
in a comic-strip balloon of antiphonal beeps,
with a virus's chemical courage, trailing a ration
of air in plexiglass and nylon, printing
a square of carbon like a tennis court,
planting our human shadow and contamination.

A hammer taps: *It is later than you think!*

                We follow
the White Rabbit through the lunar asparagus,
gathering specimens for the radiologist, peer
into the pockets of Alice's pinafore, grown infinitesimal,
fall into the daydream of the hookah and the caterpillar
and the Sea of Tears.

        Still something haunts us from that other life—
di Chirico's light, Dali's pebble seen at six o'clock,
our radical loneliness, our bereavement, our
conspiratorial nostalgia for transcendence. We hear
volcanic tumblers turning in the rock, walk
toward the blinded mirror's other side, and:

                "Do not die!"
we say. "Old fire-eater, huntress, menstrual mother,
do not die!
        See—we bring you a feather
from that other life, an answering mirror to take
the living exhalation of your breath!"

              And wait
by the deathbed for an acknowledging eye
to open, as Wordsworth's children did:

A "simple
Child that feels its life in every limb,"
(the poet said):

"What should it know of death?"

The Orphaning

1. *A Failed Rage*

Clear Idiot, I understand.

          The adversary
need not be struck, or the blow
returned. Your foreknowledge of the deed
is enough, and proves mighty. You named it Innocency:
the receptive faculty, the negative power, and wore it
under the recoil of the loved hand and the hated hand
falling equally, falling always. You said:
"Yes, I know. The blow comes as I knew it would come.
I foresaw it all. I am not angry." You turned
into your secrecy, smiled for a world's
perfidy, and denied yourself the act.

                    All this was false!
The act alone is innocent, and sweetens.
The child strikes with his fist in the womb's haven
and the father replies with the lover's spasm. Spend!
Reply! What was kept has betrayed you. See:
the rage fails, the restorative rage, and the hate
talks with its cause over the infamous pit,
touching nothing.
          Your awkwardness with tools, all
the gear of action, your poor record at the shooting range,
are the fruit of a denial. Raise the gun to your shoulder.
It is heavier than you knew. Slam the bolt to.
It will not lock to your blow.

Only what is given, is. Only the act returns.

                    Be returned.

2. *Ash Mound*

It is time you named your enemy.

Your instruments have devoured you: the poem,
the kiss, the loss, the image, the afterthought,
the orphan in the disinfected playground
crying: *Integrity!* like Job on the ash mound.

Your compass moved upon Self, always, as on a dial,
when you thought to pass beyond it,
magnetic to your incompletion. "Choice"
was a compass's fiction, and "Control,"
only the needle's need to point to the Self
when Another beckoned beyond,
and tremble to a standstill there. Always
volition lay outside, deep in the play of the act
itself—free, bold, availing, neither enemy
nor friend, partial or entire, chosen or compelled.

3. A Gift of Light

Mother, in that darkness into which you go,
which is not Lear's or Homer's—not Charon's
bowsprit bearing the devious Florentine
on the downward eddy to allegorical heaven:
nothing dreamt or dissembled, or given the spirit to know,
to prove it precarious, like thirst or the gift of tears,
but blindness itself, a smashing of lenses and lives—
why does my childhood tremble, and my gaze go up
with a child's assurance, for the large, loved hand
of that providing walker who measures her stride to my own
and steadies the balances?
                            For I guess at a thing
not desolation's, and walk, as toward birthdays, with
all my surprise made ready.

                            You come with a gift of light,
mulish and brave, in the shine of sabbatical
candles, wearing my blindness: not
in the barbiturate sleep of the maimed, but held in the salt
of a photograph, parting conventional hedges, a rich braid caught
on the serious smile and the Ukrainian stance,
by an apron of porches.

                            And all is returned in a dazzle, half
seen, like the eyelash's arc on the eye when the sleeper wakens.
Poppyseed burns on my lips. We mount up the kiosk
together, my trust in your hand like a forfeit,
climbing the steps of my nausea
while the bell-tower tips toward the dial of the orphanage

clock, and the iron opens outward.

>   There, all my sullen deprival
surrenders its lonely disguises.
>   There is my father,
clear in the long halation; there, the ascending staves of the bed,
harplike, in peeling enamel, where I listen to prodigies:
>   there,

graveplot, headstone, prayer shawl,
where the Son of the Blessing arises,
the sevenfold tape on his forearm, and remembers the prayer for the dead.

A stone in the grave of my mouth moves
and I cry from the grave-clout:
>   *Father!*

and forgive him his dying, who knew not what he did.

4. *Wedding Dance*

In the Home for the Blind
the ramps plunge under their double harness of rails
like a gymnast's parallels

or a ballerina's barre, to call the blind outdoors
and tilt them toward the gardens. There,
in the tinny brilliance and the braille

of grassy quadrants, my mother waits by the burnished iron
like a dancer by her glass, for the ticking cane,
the cuff-links and the cloth of her blinded dancing partner

that draws her failing balance
toward his arm, opens a lane in soiled, suburban air,
and guides her broken footing through the dance.

The space is full of rings,
thresholds, spikes of flying nylon, dangerous metal,
falls on the netted causeways underneath the swings,

as my mother tries her toe-hold on the wire,
prehensile as a sea-bird, breaks out a blind
umbrella, and rides the blazing slant into her *shtetl*.

She has her heart's desire
again—the moon and the fiddle, the night-skies
of Chagall, whirled on the thermal currents toward the rafters

in a bridegroom's *pas-de-deux*,
past Dante's second circle and Abraham's laughter:
"Shall Sara, that is ninety years old, bear?"

My mother holds the tightwire
like a plummet. Her partner, at his ease,
levels the pure progressions of his arc

and tops the trees! His cuff-links glint in the sun. All
is impeccable: the star-turn of the happy aerialist,
flier and flier caught on a stilled trapeze,

till the air is suddenly darker, a wind blows
cold from the used graveyard where, out of my father's eyes,
I watch the dancers print the burnt grass and move into the shadows.

5. *A Stone Raised*

When you turned from us, in your coma,
and we fought on the terrible starch of your bed
to contain your wracked pulsebeat in our circle
of unspoken bereavement,
I heard a sound like the breaking of ash in a crater
where once, in the watersheds
binding my breath to your breast,
knees to my chin,
I slept under your heart—
                    and I broke from the circle
and said:

          "Put me out of your mind. Put on your death.
          Rest. Grief cannot matter
          in the long degradation
          of blindness, maimed memory lost
          to itself, the great
          faultings of love by which the living interpret
          trespass and probity—all that forces your spirit
          to sweat in the flint and the trash of the earth like a slave

to win us survival. Take
up your bed and your grave
and walk forth to your peace."

Now I would reckon
the whole cost of our greed,
who would have the dead with us—
alive to us only in the indecent duress of their breathing—
because they still work in our pulses.

How much better that the lost and unseeing
should see through our need, in the end, foretell
our heart's changes, pass on to non-being
knowing all would be well with us!

All is well with me, Mother.

Holding the great shell of your heart
in my hands, I hear the whole power of its passion
move through my fears, with its buoys and its bells
in a tilting horizon of undertow:

your blood and your milk still encompass me.
You walk through the gums and the leaves of midsummer
first at the gates of my Sunday, with a paper
cornucopia under each hand:

There is nothing to own or disown,
nothing left to commemorate,
as now, in the year of your wish,
filling the sky like a birthmark or a ripened placenta,
knowing the rite to be good,
I bend toward your death with this stone.

IV
The Enemy Joy
(1955–1964)

How we squandered that ruin of fathers,
And how the inexhaustible fathers restore us!

The Hornet's House

Upside-down on their millstone, the hornets had already begun
That labor for slaves, oblique
Under balancing weights, where their universe hung by a wick,
Till the will of their species was done.

No longer honing their spurs under thorny abdomens
And fording the midsummer, they canted their wings on a slum
Of old parchment, a wafer of smashed candelabrum,
Unweaving and weaving their omens.

Leant to invisible headbands, hods
Of invisible chalk and saliva, some instinct alert to their need,
Had narrowed their compass to this: assembled them out of the gases, like seed
On a sunflower pod.

I thought of those others: the bee in his ziggurat, ascending
In savory waxes; the wasp turning his pouch like a fig,
Forcing the rind of his world, like the white and the shell of an egg,
In a pendant's papyrus.

But these, knowing nothing of resins, the Chaldean increases
Of stars in the hexagon, the bells of beneficent amber—
What bounty could kindle their flint in the spoors and the cinder
Of the underground places?

Yet the horn and the needle palpated, made trial
Of their hungers, till a harvest was drawn through their bellies,
Rode like the thread in an hourglass, a stinger of waxes and jellies,
And struck in consummate denial

Till everything blazed like a thought, like a sexual breathing of gauzes,
While a kingdom of predators, circling, put forth its antennas,
And the poem arose like a hornet, in rabbinical blacks and siennas,
On craters and crosses.

Second Adam

Whatsoever Adam called every living creature, that
was the name therof.   —Genesis

When the Deluge had passed,
into my head, by twos, came the creeping things,
the horn of their jawbones shining, and the things of the air,
wing-cases breaking like clasp knives, asking their names.

Storm-light colored their passing
with an animal imminence. They wheeled
on the pile of their plumage, in the dread of their animal being,
and rode in the ark of my head

where the possible worked like a sea.
Nothing was given me there. Nothing was known. Feather and scale,
concussions of muscle and fur, the whale and the name for the whale
rose on the void like a waterspout, being, and ceasing to be:

till keel clashed and I spoke: *mayfly,*
wood-weasel, stingray, cormorant, mole—
choosing the syllables, holding a leaf to the torrent,
unharmed and infallible, while Creation descended, in twos.

A Salamander Seen

Salamander
that speaks of our wonder in caustic Sumerian;
whose movement
tilting the summer a moment,
opens a scar in the mica
and stings like the blade of an adze—

serpent that lives in my doubt
on the animal edge of that leap
where the poised and the possible,
nude as a pulse in the sun,
enters the holocaust's ray, breathes upon stone
and sleeps where the darknesses are—

whose depths are the desert
and the whole of that innocence
that smiles at opacity and breaks from the mineral
spray, a dolphin of quicklime and air—

nearer to me than my heartbeat, subtle as frost—

angel of impulse
that leans on its saurian fingers,
abstract beyond pathos; that
eludes the intent of my joy

and is lost.

The Cremation: New Mexico

(for Eda Lou Walton)

I burn a slight body
placelessly left in my mind, as best I can:
the flower on a cactus's thistle should do it,
or the wilderness fan
where cloudbursts ride on a Conestoga wheel
in summer electric, storm over storm, in a bitter braking of iron.

But a marvel is worked in the sun. The light
that a boy might point with a burning-glass,
singeing the distance with a deckle of papery rust
or curling the print where the smoke of the stylus passes—
carbon and gossamer—poised upon your dying,
masses like Indian turquoise for your ghost.

Your country
breathes in a lion's slumber:
O rise on that furnace of claws
in the bestiaries of your Armageddon,
enter your desolation and your angers,
and walk to Abraham's bosom, through the paws.

Court of the Lions: Alhambra

(Granada)

For the monster's simplicity, the menacer's
Way to the center—what but a labyrinth?

The hieratic lions of Alhambra
Circle the court like a map-maker's rose,
In a poodle-dog's tonsure, ferocious, solicitous,
Their muzzles, bared for the waterspout,
Four times scored with a grimace,
Their manes on their powerless shoulders, like a fleece,
Taking the basin's weight on their trumpery toes
Among cameras, talismans, Baedekers, legendary gesso.

Only the lions keep simple.

                    In the labyrinth's center,
They honor a myth of the instinct's simplicity
With a monster's indifference.

                    Their savage vocation,
Among pentagrams, figured cartouches, ceremonial plaster:
To humble the conjuror and mock the enchanter
With the unreflective revelation of the obvious.
The minotaur's rhetoric
And all the apparatus of the maze
Fails on their barbarous haunches
And melts in the runneling marble
                        Whatever
Has blazoned the arches with calligrams, pomegranates, eight-pointed stars,
Feathered the mortar
With the peacock's extravagance, surrenders its sorcery
Here in the lion's enclosure.
                      Here, the invisible ringmaster
That levels the hoop of the fountain's periphery
And lashes a length of cautionary water,
Would have them pigeon-breasted, plaintive, and apparent.

Yet they speak for a fable's conclusion. They prepare
For the bestial deliverer:

          "The wands of the Eastern geometer
Are splintered like straw," say the lions. "The cult of the djinn
    and the scarab,
The construers of entrails, wishing-bone addicts, compounders
Of formulas, philtres, phylacteries, plain and quadratic equations,
Bow to the lions.
              Here, on the portico table,
The kingdom of nuance, the fiends of inhuman refinement
Bend to the fallible animal. Here
The Christian intercessors of our passion,
Armed with an outcry, immediate as a stutter,
Attended by lions, strike through the net and the trident
And batter the skulls of the Arab. . . ."

                      So say the lions:
While, on their amenable quarters,
The water falls delicate, the enchanter's enigma arises,
Plane over plane and diamond into diamond,
Bossing the surfaces, starring the grain of the panels
With the poet's *Kasidah*,*
                 multiplying columns.

For the place of the beast is bewitched, say the lions.
                        The channels
Are stained with the blood of a prince's vendetta.
The fountain's thread descends to Evangelist's navel
And charms like a hypnotist's prism.

                  See; even the marble devises
A sleep for the lions! Whatever their vigil,
Poem and magic are joined in a dream for a savage's pleasure.
Alhambra assembles
Its ascending wasp-nest's heaven
Pouched in the plummeting chalks twenty ways planed
To the ceiling's improbable vertex, like a leaven;
Its columns in harvest clusters, ringed
On the marble's shewbread; in a Musselman script
Cursive and flourishing, repeating a violent fable
In the semblance of bowsprits, wheat-staves, cutlasses,
Hummingbird vibrations.

Kasidah: Arabic verse-form incorporated among the geometric and floral motifs
by the Alhambra architects.

Battle-Piece

(Uccello's "Battaglia di San Romano")

1. *After Uccello*

I have fought that battle in heraldic panels
Bitten in leathers, in Uccello's image
Under the poising and the leveling lances
Crossing the visors and trumpets.
      I have seen,
In a hedgehog's vigil, ceremonious slaughter:
Halberd on battle-mace, crossbows tight on their jesses
With a hawk's extension, the rider's face
Bowed to his horse's mane under favors and feathers,
His profile naked to hazard in a locust's weight of armor.

What the fighting portended,
Or how, in a spoiled light, that leaden
Discomfiture darkened our spearpoints, the guidons
Failed on their silks, and the drum-skin's hoop grew tauter,
No one remembers.
      The maps and the outriders
Gave us no notice. The champion,
Sighting his lance's length in an umber perspective,
Awaited some sunburst to blazon that burden of armor
And interpret the contest's directive.

        Nothing responded.

2. *Another Part of the Field*

An unsuitable landscape, surely.

       Commanded
And chosen at once; inhuman and intimate, fated,
Familiar:
   the light of apocalypse
Forced through the smoke of a burning-glass,
Bitumen and nimbus together.
       In the distance,
The hearth-beds of millet in a harrowed and featureless
Valley, the brand of the husbandman's furrow,
Rose vertical.

Pomegranates reddened
The leafage—an eclipse's corona—yet the season
Was iron: a furnace's floor where no holocaust was:

And the time was Armageddon.

3. *Encounter*

The spur spins. The contender
Spins on the cinch's wheel of his saddle.

                                                 He measures necessity
With a pikestaff's haft, from his wish's circumference
To the center of violence.
                             Fatality flows
Down his pikestaff's length
To the curve of his bannerol. He touches the barb
To his pulses, steadies
The shaft on a corselet of nerves.
                            And is ready.

While that antagonist
On the belled Arabian crop of his stallion,
In a turban's swathe, his lance
On the pin of his elbow like the hub of a compass,
Forces mortality's sweat drop.

The spur spins, the contender
Spins on the dial of his saddle:

                        And the contest begins.

4. *A Reading of Entrails*

When the omens were served, we withdrew
To a higher position.

                      We prepared for the reading of entrails.

We saw that the mottoes were struck
On a grave-keeper's cradle-song. The champion's
Shock on the champion, the decorum of armies,
The breaching of metal and adamant, breastplate and barbican,
Were one to the sybil.

The portent that orders all circumstance
Descends in a bloodbath, and legend is changed into chance.

But a legend was served!
Whatever the omens portended
Or the weapon sought to refine to its satisfaction—
The bowmen debouched in the appointed valley,
The paladin's silks went up with the angry devices,
Emblem and ikon yellowed the embroidered borders
Defender measured the field with the defended,
And all was ordered
As in a decoration by Uccello:

A foreground of horses:
turquoise and cinnamon shod
With a jeweler's crescent; the straining albino,
His contemplative chessman's head in his bridle's rosette
Calm in the contact of riders.
A navy of javelins
On the overturned horses—a carousel's
Splintered rotations:
the field of the wilderness cinder
Fixed in its fated relations like an armorer's fable:
The House of the Rod and the Water-Bow, the Cresset, the Sheaf
and the Gryphon—

The cinquefoil thicket laced with a pollen of poppies

The dismounted anonymous god in the goldleaf rubble—

And circling him there, on the broken lunette of his shield:
Three hares
and a greyhound pursuing
and the invisible thong of the snare.

5. *Festival of Anger*

One, with a trident, in the stable's
Ammoniac dung waits for the bluefly's epiphany; one
Turns from the watery burnish, the millennial
Barrow that honors a monster,
And enters a labyrinth; one, in a havoc of horses,
Harrows the world's rage with his lance's point
For a chapel, a chalice, the cannibal kiss of a brother.

105

Fighters in the blood, contenders
Antlered or garlanded, horned and necessitous ones—
Old changelings of the gorged heart of the toad
Who come by ways as desperate as this
To work in the breastbone and whiten the cicatrix:
However we sham or subvert the indifferent disaster
Or give the ungratified godhead of the scourge
The service of the sedulous offender,
Your angers are festive!

                    Yours but to touch
The tinder to the tinder, the inexpressive
Desert adamant that hardens its venom
In the forge of the cactus,
And has no thought of sacrilege or pardons,
Incense, oblations, or talismanic letters:
                             that breaks
The providential fountain from the stone
And looks like history or hope, but takes
A moment's inadvertence for its own.

I would fight that battle after the battle,
Inward and naked, after the outward
Packs like a weaver's spindle or poises like a picture
Baroque with the ceremonious violence of the shuttle,
The pencil, the burin, the matched and extortionate word—
The battle of the monster and the mothers
That no contender wages for a legend
At a charmed lake's bottom;
                      where nothing moves, but the imagining
Begetter and the habitual figures of his quarrel—
Who sees, beyond the landscape of surrender,
The pomegranates redden in a pomp of laurel,
The furrow blazing like a revelation—

And circling him there, still placeless and unimagined,
Three hares
           and a greyhound pursuing
                      and the invisible thong of the snare.

Lives of Mrs. Gale

1. Death and the Next of Kin

My pity followed your plaid back, into the sun, to the car
in a holocaust that would rattle you home
from the furniture oil and detergents and the splintering
telephone bell in the vacuum's hoses,
to your porch in South Shaftsbury.

                    There, by the cutouts of poodle
and duck in the flowering pig-dirt, the cast-iron cat on the maple
flashing its egg-yolk enamels, the denims and doilies,
Puss-in-Boots in a pinafore tinted in tripes and molasses
on tinfoil, Roy and his bottle—the Unthinkable struck.
The hairs of your head stood on end. And at last,
in the sweat of your glasses,
                    you wept.

2. Death and the Seventh Son

A seventh son, or a last—
however you reckoned it:

                    The boy in the bulldozer
never needing you less, the untender; the wayward
and quarrelsome father and unwitting
offender, out of love with the Law, straddling
a cloud with an aerial to pleasure
your Sundays; easy with tears,
                    like yourself . . .

On your way to the Hospital, with the face in the oxygen
bag come closer, some things fell together:
Bertie and Isobel, runaways. The smash-up
near White River. Sticks and a star
in a soldier's necropolis. Arthritical weather,
with the well-drillers gouging the gardens, and the water
at two hundred feet showing gritty—

                    No use to harden
the heart or take on!
              If the answer was bitter—
something you'd done, something you'd found and forgotten, well

that was for later—the more was the pity!
But it all added up into *Cancer*.

3. *Death Watch*

In the wallpaper jungle, with the stove
snuffling lamp-oil and the living-room crammed with a death,
the question resumed.

          The death of a son is momentous.
It gathers the glaze in linoleum
parlors, blues the laces with starches, hardens
the nooses of neckties and buttons up collars,
and waits for our love, like a service.

              The Thing that was meant—the framed
face in the oval that looked toward the face in the casket
where the range of the Thinkable crashed on a death-date—

hostile alike to consent and forgiveness—
                   wanting only
denial—

     a Vermonter would know how to choose between sugar
and granite.

     And the death of a son needed granite.

4. *The Beast in the Quarry*

That quarry in Danby!

          The blocks came out smoking
with spray and acetylene. The heft of a mountain, the electric
and diamond of drillers, the marks of its anger were on it.
One could picnic on granite. Cobble pathways. And in June,
in the melted abysses, where the terrible adamant mounted
or fell, out of birch into fire, one could dive toward the time of a planet.

It was marble—the negations of marble—that counted!

So you strove with that sleepy destroyer in the maw
of the quarry where a season lay locked in its guilty

mutations.

        The spider-plant greened on the window.

                                   The ground-thaw

worked on the slate in the pit of the well, a pillar
of drouth in the garden, the cats, and the crosses.

Denial and pain were made perfect.

                    And two summers later,

after the lawyers and losses,
the water came up.

         It rose three hundred feet

in the main, breaking strong in the pipe-elbows.

                        For the first time

the tap in your kitchen ran

            hot and cold,

               your weariness bathed

to its length in a porcelain tub.

               And the taste of the water was sweet.

The Lightning-Rod Man

(for Howard Nemerov)

1. Calligrams

Your Chinese poets in a jovial dynasty
would have ordered things otherwise:
                              two rhyming topers
sculling in lotus pods in a casual dory,
stopped by a calligram:
                              a scallop of water
on a carp's fin, with a brightening
fish-scale laid over, like a riddle in Mandarin—
frightening, perhaps, and premonitory,
saying: *Moon of ancestral Destroyer: think about drowning* . . .

Or it is Melville: The Lightning-Rod Man in green glass
and copper, topped with three tines, like a hearth-god
in Pittsfield:
            "Sir, have you ever been *struck?*
There are no castles in thunderstorms. Mine is the only
true rod. A dollar a foot. Proceed with precaution. Avoid
pine trees and lonely Kentuckians, steel sashes and bell-pulls.
                                                      Your man
is a proper conductor. The lightning goes into and out of a man—
but a tree is peeled clean, like a pineapple.
                              Don't push your luck."

2. A Look at Lightning

The bolt, taking the line of the poplar
in the shirkshire,* slammed past the bark
through runneling leaves, found an an angle of shingle
and smashed through the clothes-closet. The desk-lamp went dark.

And *worked* in that room: a methodical killer
smelling of flint and burnt almond, cotton-gloved
like a safe-cracker, cutting wires, picking tumblers,
moving over my letters, the things I had hoarded or loved:

A wind of exceptional violence, often followed by rain. Regional: Bennington Valley, Vermont.

Old pesos. Indian pennies. Loose change
in a jar from Gibraltar. Postcards from Pompeii in unplaceable
reds; a cosmetic of garlands and winged *amorini*
in blood-rust and ashes, to prefigure the strange

and erotic where the bolt worked before. Still tracking copper,
it rode in the wiring like punk, exploded in plaster and rubble,
blackened a voice in the radio tube on its way to a fortunate
answer, and spelled out in Nineveh: *trouble!*

3. *Second Lightning*

Ah, but that other time!

                 The forecasts, the starlings
that fly in the pulp of the weather maps,
were bland, to the zenith.
                 Cruciform in a garden,
I lay in the sunbather's negative world, in the dark
of my glasses, in the dream of a camera's
reversals:
           blackest of all at the sun,
black where the light turns on hipbone and haunches,
black to the pit of the eyeball where a feather of shadow
shuts out the stun and the brilliance.

                     Something struck
through the terrible gases, a fasces of flames
in a fist, at my brain and my blood and my sex,
rode through the locks of the orphanage door
where my childhood looked up from the salt and the clocks
of a playground, a drill field, a courtyard, noon milk
in a cup, a graveyard of cots, a latrine.
The thunder began, the unplaceable red in the green,
I saw the tines blaze on the head of the Lightning-Rod Man:
and I ran—

         toward the Drum-Room, the Drummer, his man's hands
on my hands on the drumsticks, guiding the sticks on the skins
while the thunder rose out of the hides to the window-bars
holding the midsummer.
                A gutter-bird sang in the tar
by the swings and the seesaws.

111

The driveway spun
with its institutional flowers, its identical
pike-staff cage and its cinder-track—
                              toward
my father, smashing clothes in a pressing machine, a daguerreotype
face looking back over ashes and the leonine
threads in the scrolls,
                    —dead and intent on his dying—
matching the seam of a trouser-leg over the seam, locking the sections,
applying the steam and the paddle

                         while the mica and iodine fell.

4. *View of Toledo*

What does the lightning intend?

                    The wish is beneficent, surely,
that bends toward such brightness to show us the shape of our terror,
or works in a cloud on a city's unpeopled perspectives—
not with the dark and the light of a sundial's gradations, but purely,
in pumice and hurricane, all at once, like a landscape of knives.

As once in Toledo:

                    a Greek, at a burial, coming nearer,
struck at the shroud of Count Orgaz, found the eschatological greens
in the rust of a cardinal's cape, the gold of the surplice's
threads—
                    rolled back the stone of his eyeballs
in the place of the skulls, and shewed us the bread of our lives.

Memorial Hospital: Outpatient

(for Dr. Oliver Durand)

Leaving that cradle of bed-baths and bells
for the hurrying mothers who summon his childhood
on the helpless enamel, he passes the doorways
again: the sealed, with the masks and the gases,
where blood learns its interval under a bubble
and the desperate climb their thermometers:

                                        the doors set ajar
for the fear like a colorless smell
in the night-light; the ward-room's windowglass cages
and graves where terror lives openly:
the aged in abbatoirs
with the ox's albuminous look; the arthritic,
alive in a fright-wig of hair by the turreted
bed-table, among juices and pepperplants—
all that threshold of pathos exploding in chemical rages,
waxworks and madhouse—the paralytic's magnesium stare
and the plotted mutations where hazard ascends and descends.

He has watched with the murdered, a casual.

                                        Now
the corridors flow by incurable quarrels,
beneficent sponges, lenses, and dyes,
bearing him back across enemy lines
in a gutter of chloroform, where the innocent,
crouched in the cave of their skulls, on the torch of their spines,
celebrate their abstinence with animal cries.

He would say something, pointing his breath like an icicle,
shamed in his appetites, taking the knife of the snow,
sleepy with certainty.

                    But already
the shipwrecks sail out on their pillow-slips,
small in their bedsheets, unforgiving,
intent on the shoreline that sparkled like salt
in his fevers.

            What would he know,
who returns with his hurt to the bran and the meat of the living?

The mothers could gather him back to the night
of their laps and speak of his fault:
but the mothers are locked under needles and crystals . . .

The car races its motor and guns down the driveway.
The pine smokes in its resins:
                              needles and crystals.

                                        There is nowhere but light.

V
Wilderness Stair
(1939–1955)

Dance Piece

". . . at the still point, there the dance is."
—T. S. Eliot

The errand into the maze,
Emblem, the heel's blow upon space,
Speak of the need and order the dancer's will.
But the dance is still.

For a surmise of rest, over the flight of the dial,
Between shock of the fall, shock of repose,
The flesh in its time delivered itself to the trial,
And rose.

Sufferance: the lapse, the pause,
Were the will of the dance—
The movement-to-be, charmed from the shifts of the chance,
Intent on its cause.

And the terrible gift
Of the gaze, blind on its zenith, the wreath
Of the throat, the body's unwearied uplift,
Unmaking and making its death,

Were ripeness, and theme for return:
Were rest, in the durance of matter:
The sleep of the musing Begetter
And the poise in the urn.

(Homage to Martha Graham)

Departures

"These things that live on departure
Understand when you praise them."
  —R. M. Rilke

1. *Vermont Quarry*

The look was never summer's
And, with an altering reason,
Nightly the maple sweetened the block at its root
And opened its chilly cisterns over pumice.
Rigors of quartz, in the delicate season,
Darkened the sheaf and emptied the apple-crystal;
And always the taste of the granite followed the taste of the fruit.

This was for the wrecked hillside to say;
For the plough, on its side in the leavening cloud
And the dazzle of stubble:
Time was the emery's, and moved, in the quarrier's way,
An inch in the vehement dark
Where spectrums ripened to trouble the point of a spark
And deepen an instant of marble.

2. *Trade Wind: Key West*

Esteban, in a musk rear room,
Turns at the blown pane and spans a clear cigar.
                                        Beyond,
A splint of mummying tinder; scarabs, fans,
Rocking the palm-glare, leaf under leaf, like rain—
                              And *there! there!*
That diminishing gust!
A guise of sails, meridian air
Bluing the Mexican floor,
Dropping the bracken garland and the herb

On verdures
              portents
                        gargoyles of coral dust;
Toppling a gull at the sand's edge, an overturned basket of cane
That leans to the ripple
                    and settles to rest
                              . . . as before . . .

3. *Tourist and Turtle: Key West*

There where the ebb gives phosphor, and begins
Its tender overturn
A fathom's depth in shale,
Under the mica gardens and the fins—

A green sojourn—

The palm, the prism, keeping an alternate myth,
Serene returns
Under the sidelong quibble of the gull:

And turtle fables, iron over pith,
That worry a marble saddle through the trough,
And try the waterline,
And rinse a mariner nostril free—
                                    and cough—
And strike a strenuous sweetness out of brine.

4. *The Sand Painters: New Mexico*

The thumb, for a summer's promise,
Leans to its shadow on the cloud-colored sand
And measures its wilderness crystal, to a line . . .

The shadow deploys, and the cloud, and the catch of the singer,
Leaving the pure stroke after the considering hand,
Wise in an animal stealth, abstemious, fine:

> *The small-headed goddess . . . fasces of hemlock and arrows . . .*
> *Miraculous sunwheel, bound in a bowcord strain . . .*
> *The side-pointing buffalo eyes in a pumice of mirrors . . .*

Returns. Recoils. The enormous web moves under.
The cloud sways westward, poising its pyramid stain.
The Spinner ascends the loom of meridian,
While, through the sift of his finger,
A thong in the hourglass trembles from thunder to thunder
And empties a season of rain.

5. *Celebrated Jumping Frog: Calaveras County*
   "Gradation, gradation—then a sudden leap."
                                           —André Gide

Bells in the valley where the sheep
Lean to the slope in the flawing snow;
And still the frogs of Calaveras keep
Athenian laughter in the quartz's sleep:
Sweetness of metal: balsam and alkali
Between the serpent's ages and the sea.

Only the human watcher waits, apart,
Smiling the blind denial of his woe—
Masquer and malcontent, bounded by a heart,
Lending the whittler's tribute of his art
To what the olive and the orange bless:
A pedant-in-a-basket, saying: *yes!*

While, with an ironist's consent,
A multiple summer flashes, from below,
The poppy and the pomegranate's intent—
Faggot of grapestock—and the leaf is bent:
And breaking from the buckshot and the bog,
The pledge is paid, that lost the jumping frog.

6. *Ditty: Moby Dick at Nantucket*

I saw, over the gun's bore this summer,
In a trick of light,
The young boats with a dazed sail
And finical spars spanned tight
To charm the inland comer
By the cropped wave with a child's guess of a whale—

And cheered, in a lucky charade,
For the white whale-hump and the Spearer,
Playing the innocent fraud
Of the Death of the Terror,
Till the sail drew nearer

And the fable went down
Under the waste dune

And the pat verge of the hedge,
And, out of the water's edge,
Rose, in the cold salt, the blue bore of the gun.

7. *Cactus Gardens: Oaxaca*

It is no common sun
That opens a collar of horn
And forces the thorn-point's ascension.
                              What is won
In the cactus's knot—
The bandolier's crescent of bullets, or the oval
That closes a god's meditation—
Strikes on the cactus's paddle
And shows, in a disk of sweat, the incendiary, salt angel.

Not that serener invention:
Our wayfarer's Lady, disclosed in a mountain cantina,
Poised upon trefoil, treading the fountains of tallow,
Her slipper's point grazing the altar-stone, haggard
With glass and perspective.

                    Not hers,
But the desert's intention:
The cactus's paddle
Unharmed in the holocaust, bone-white on tin:
The wilderness mercy reversed in a brazen arena
Scored with the cactus's fiber:
The fronds of unfailing maguey
That take the mirage of the world and burnish all distance to one:

This way, the sun-burst of thorn, that way, the thorn-burst of sun.

8. *Bull-Ring: Plaza Mexico*

In the funnel's baroque
Where dark and light, like axeblades facing,
Mimicked the murderer's stroke:
The bull's double peak and the decimal spacing
Of twinned banderillas—*two and two and two*—
The yoke of magenta and maize on the holocaust's field; and below,
The breathing of Samson, in a cable of lather and spittle.

His death gave to the blackening ring
More than the hilt at rest in a column of gristle
Or the agonist's warlock shared in a multitude's shadow—
Gave fear, in the hump where the rapier rode, without anger,
Odor of milk and lament, the wafer and manger,
The cape's corolla and the ruining Spring

And Dionysus drowsing in a meadow.

9. *Near Iguala: Market*
   "Is good, joven?"

The shadower bears
Wicker of sweet savor: the festival bread
And the orange's cusp on his head.

                                        Early
The bandages rise over pestilent cobble
For the awning's asylum. Color will spread
In the trophy of ice,
The pomegranate bleed under leather;
And carnage's midday will gather
The worm on the tine of the skewer and the rind in the rubble.

But morning is ample . . . Dynamite. Bells.
The tiles' ablution in a running of ochre and blood.
A dinting of blueness—
The hammer on silver—the stranger's mnemonic of smells.

A wire in the wood
Practices yesterday's tenderness.
                                        Dewless,
The burro ascends in a garland of flies.
The cupola's noon is forever.

                     "Is good!"

10. *Valley of Virginia*
    (for Evelina O. Wiggins)

The bird's round, begun
In dogwood's mortality, in the pit of the petal's serration,

Fails, to our hazard. Whatever the casuist sang
To lighten a planet's momentum or charm our mistrust—
The dogwood is edged with a fang
And prepares its corruptible property: a crescent of rust
In the terrible oxide of sun.

For praise's vocation,
What but the heart's whole charity? The dogwood
Fails, to our hazard, if color
Harden my brother's darkness, like a scar,
And trothless in midsummer's valor
The trout drives Noah's rainbow through the water
And mockingbird says: *daystar . . . daystar . . .*

11. *Cricket Hill: Vermont*

> *"Place there is none; we go backward and forward, and there is no place."*
>
> —Saint Augustine

The wish brought me, at last,
To country shingle under a panic cloud,
Where, from the field's edge, under my heart's dead weight,
Over the bells of fodder and the slate,
The steep rain struck and aerial tinders passed
And the harrow's crescent, bloody with idleness, showed.

There, the unsmiling providence of the year
Gathered the extravagant blazons of its loss:
The apple's defection, genius of vinegar,
Struck on the whirling fly; the spine and the stalk;
Axe-helve and trident; spoilure and overplus—
And rose in the horn and richened its husk; *and broke!*

And moved, in the cricket's interval of pause,
Bearing the blazing rondure of a season
Toward those enormous countries of the center
That open a side and bid the intruder enter,
Tilting a marble cusp to the horizon
And binding a doomed occasion to its cause.

And, in the wish's kingdom of completion,
Departure's placename beckoned toward no-place

123

And the expressive passion smiled upon its source:
The nude head yielded, ringed in its clear halation;
Prism and lash moved down; the kiss
Fell and grew great, struck, and was universe.

Karamazov

1. *Smerdyakov with a Guitar*
> *"Who doesn't wish his father dead?"*—Ivan Karamazov

I looked from the stairwell.

                The scream
Of the feigned fall whirred in my throat,
No longer dissembled, and my mother arose from the dung
Big with my outrage.
               The cellar-door swung . . .

And I moved through an epilept's dream:
A guitar and a melon, floretted, a noose and a fang,
A cradle that pulsed like a heart and a crystal that sprang,
Showing my father asleep in his spilth in a streamer of gall,
His nakedness sparkling like alcohol . . .

And I lifted my birth, like a jawbone:
                  "Is it now, Mother?"
I called to the stairwell: *"Mother, do we tumble him now?"*

—The melon-rind tightened. The strings of the fingerboard trembled—

And: *"Murderer!"* came in the pause. *"Would you murder the Husbandman? Bow!
Bow!"* said my mother: *"Bow down to the innocent Cause!"*

So I beat on the rind with my jawbone
                    and bowed to my father

And sang.

2. *Alyosha's Funeral Service*
> *"Instead of lenten oil, I will give you sucking pig and kasha."*
> —Karamazov

If the child's tooth
Fall on the unoffending finger, the finger
Bleeds for it, and the stone shows blood.

I am content with that.
               It suffices for crucifixion.

It was corruption's smell that led me to my father,
A carrion way through the saint's phosphorescence
And the faulting mind of my brother, to the incorruptible Presence,
Where, at the horn's end, awaiting the idiot Bringer,
A child's death babbles of dogs in an innocent fiction
And all things acknowledge the dissolute beast of the good.

Construe, little pigeons:
How we squandered that ruin of fathers,
And how the inexhaustible fathers restore us!

Old liars, dividing the verities,
Broken-haired mountebanks, eaters of cabbage and gudgeon,
Snoring in spittle and driving their murders before us,
Gods of the pestle and mortar and priests of the bludgeon,
Touching their thighs in an augury, and looking like youth—

Where was an end to their love?

                        When our violence faltered,
They contrived the empowering outrage to bloody our knuckles
And accomplish their perfect destruction.
When we rose on the smoke of the sacrifice, vaunting our famine,
Fasted and absolute, crackling the crystals of salt,
They broke the abysses and showed us the bladders of salmon
Sowing the deluge like pollen.

                        Their benevolence altered
The zenith's unsparing progressions and the span of the sickle,
Calling the figures of dread and credulity up
And shaping the seasons' similitudes for the lover:

The thread of the mayflower, beforehand, stilting a cup
On the scrolled leaf and the imminent foils of summer;
The skunk in the shorn grass, in chicory and clover,
Forcing his whiteness under a ringing of stars;
The moth in a pathos of veins
                        cadaver of perishing color . . .

In whatever defiled or affronted us—
The coveter's rage that we dreamed on the beds of our neighbors,
Crimes, contradictions, enigmas, anomalies, wars,
Chance's inspired alternations at play with the possible,
Perfidies, nightmares, vendettas—
                        they haunted us,

Demanding a parricide's justice to hallow their labors
And work the design of their voices.

Their gift was dismay and unreason: the saving enormity
That heeled on its instincts and bayed its intent, like a dog,
Grinding the gristle and bone of the spirit's deformity
And pursuing its will-to-perfection into the bog.

For their need was profane, like our own—

                                 a dream of abundance
In the lewd cornucopia's helix that bounds the abyss
And whirls the extremes of our will on its blinding redundance:
The rout of the priest and the scribe and the epilept beggar,
Beads, lacerations, and martyrdoms—
                                   Armageddons, gardens . . .
The equivocal vision of judgment concealed in a parable
Where the intriguer's coffin waits, and the intriguer,
Forever uninnocent, sways toward the terrible wardens,
While over the leveling rifles,
A rider approaches upon the inquisitor's errand,
Bearing the pardon that murders, and the murder that pardons.

The Habit of Angels

1. *Jacob and His Angel*
   "I will not let thee go, except thou bless me."

Contest, the habit of angels,
Tempted the man from the wilderness stair.
He rose from his dream of the sheaves and the climbing evangels
And clasped his antagonist there.

And tasting his want in the ritual's enterprise,
He swayed on the blaze of that shoulder and emptied his strength
And saw (it may be) in the ring of the combatant's eyes
The ladder's verge, at length.

What sued for the blessing and humbled the angel's election
Was known to his brother: a carnival cheat of the shell,
A modern advantage that purchased an omen's perfection
And cozened the boy from the well,

And drew, in the chance of the pit, the guile of the dreamer,
The blood-clabbered god in the road backdrawn by the hair:
The bounty of Egypt, the thrift of the merchant-redeemer,
The void at the sheer of the stair.

2. *Lamentation of Job*
   *"And he took himself a potsherd to scrape himself withal and he
   sat among the ashes."*

Was it to startle the Adversary in His own element
That that good man opened the doorway of his flesh
And measured his body's rebellion with the tempter's intent
In a figure of ash?

The havens of Shaddai, the oils of the assuager
Bled, with the ministering potsherd, for this man
As again, in the cynical service of the wager
The afflictions of Egypt began:

Ravage of children and the root's betrayal,
Marrow's infirmity and the sickening air,
Havoc and canker, murrain and massacre
And all the maniac rhetoric of denial.

But most, when the intellectual justice of the city
Darkened his loss with the grasshopper's counsel, and killed,
And spoke in the Comforters' comedy of pity
The hero's despair was fulfilled—

Who saw that the tempters were three, and their solace,
Adam's contagion in the ghost's beginning:
Defeat of awe, millenniums of cunning,
And the syllogist's malice.

And, in the place of the rock and the ladder where a godhead faded
And all the inheritors of Jesse slept
He watched while a pustule gathered . . . Almost, he was persuaded,
And therefore Job wept.

3. *Another Sorrowing Woman*
     "Woman, what have I to do with thee?"

I have willed the event,
At length, and confront the violent shape,
And break, on the pyx of my lap,
In the old, paschal posture, the obscene Innocent.

The pure vocation of that younger rage—
Godhead, little with woe—
Must bend to the stone of my knees and take its wage
And measure that murderous anvil, for the blow—

And die, for a mourning animal
In a schoolboy's subterfuge of grief.
Taking the expedient kiss, the coronal
Maudlin with thorns, between the deaths of a thief.

Playfellow: go. It is the old exchange,
The Roman platitude;
And it shall leave you range
To puzzle, again, your pedant's idea of the good
In a child's solitude.

     (after Michelangelo's "Pietà")

4. *Goliath Stone*

"Let all things that have breath praise the Lord."

What stayed, was the wish to praise
In a causeless occasion.

The wasp in the throughshine, by the unreal window,
Above scarabs, in the termite's detonation,
Snored on the blind glaze, brightened a shard,
And opened the hallowing summer of its pulses.

He saw the blessed hem close on the approaching sandal,
The bland linen scrolled with a double vector,
The fringe, the sponge,
The big hands in the harp's transparencies
Tensing the sling-stone, with knuckles starred,
The lifeline pierced with the suppliant's fingernail—

The vexed head in its armory—

The nostril's volute in the beard's foil—

And under the crown's weight, the stone's three distances:
Absolom, Jonathan, Saul.

Soundstage

(U.S. Signal Corps Photographic Center: 1945)

1.

Catwalk, backdrop, cable, girder, fly—
A schooner capsized.

                      Sea-fans of artifice
Buoyed in the middle currents; gelatin and foil;
Baskets of radiant cordage; geysers of frost;
Miraculous canvas in the glowing levels, glazed,
The backdrops weedy, like oil . . .

                            The ropes plunge and are lost;
Are parted like hair,
Where, at the summit, among crucibles of light,
Equilibrist Gulliver
Calls to the carpenters in a tightwire vertigo,
At the Archimedean center of deception, unamazed.

And all that is, is film. Film is
The serpent in Eden garden, the cord in the chrysalis,
The bough in the dove's beak, trying the Deluge,
The thread in the labyrinth,
The Great Wall of China spanning the dynasties
Like a calligraphic symbol; meridians, staves
Between the upper and the nether icecaps; trajectory
Of shell and tracer bullet, phosphor and satchel-charge;

The looped *l* given to the paper poorly on the burning tripod

And the victory over horror in an image.

2.

The boy in the uniform of Oberleutnant, the demoniac flier,
Will not bleed humanly from the papier-mâché doorway.
                                     The door
Will not close truly on the plausible flight,
With leisure for vanity, vacancy, mania, the stunned recognition.
And mocking the human wish for asylum,
Spray-gun and saw, the jaw of the plier,
Have outpaced fable.

It is divertissement, after all.

What is stilted in canvas, jailed to the plywood wall,
Stabbed to the floor
With wing-screws and metal angles,
Melts into vaudeville in a whirr of velocipedes
And a yelping of trained poodles,
A swindle of spangles.
Only the scaffold gives stress to the weightless interior
On the wrong side of the pattern: the artisan's touch of the actual.

3.

Yet teased out of thought,
The smiling divination of the Spool
Whirls forever in the large eye of Keats, heavy with film.
For even that Attic shape,
The bride of quietness brought to bed on the urn,
Was not more actual than this.
                                        And, in equivocal distance,
Necessitous armies close, image and spectacle wait
And beat on the canvas door;
The fiction
Calls in the camera's crystal to existence,
Loud as myself—

                    in deed, in ghost—

And bleeds in Agamemnon's color,
And is articulate.

The Spool

They splay at a bend of the road, rifles slung, the
shadows minimal, their hands tugging their slings by
the upper swivel to ease the routine of the march.
They have been moving since morning, and over each
has descended that singleness, mournful and
comatose, which is the mysterious gift of the march.
Their helmets shadow their eyes, their chinstraps
dangling. In the raddle of grasses their solitude
floats in a drift of identities, a common melancholy.

A captain enters the frame at the head of his
company. His face flashes. With his left hand he tilts
back his helmet, while with his right he draws the
length of an elbow across forehead and nose, his
stained armpits showing dark. A bracelet flashes
behind him. The column recedes, rifles close over the
canted belts, moving up, the packed backs vulnerable:

(Cut)

Late afternoon. In the halflight a handful of blazing
sticks, four infantrymen heating mess tins over an
eddy of smoke, a fifth on his hams, his eyes upcast
from the rim of his metal cup. Nearby a corporal
works a patch into the chamber of his rifle;
he repeats four syllables and smiles sleepily into
the camera. The camera moves to the bivouac area;
a group, their meatcans close to their mouths,
spooning the compost, Chinese-fashion, and clowning
between mouthfuls. Very close. Their jaws,
lightly bearded, the necks in their jacket collars
strained in an easy horseplay, the Adam's apples
rapidly raised and released in the human exertion
of eating. In deep shadow, the light failing,
very close. A private tugs at his boot by the toe
and the round of the heel. Deliberately, he draws
the boot clear of his foot, sets it aside with deep
satisfaction, massages his instep over a maternal
thickness of socks. He bends toward the other foot,
camera-shy, a half-smile breaking;

(Cut)

It is not yet possible to distinguish the forms

behind the camouflage netting. They move in the
central darkness of the gun, stacking shells and
bringing up powder charges. Only the bulk of the
howitzer is sure, the gun-barrel crossing the line
of the valley under the tented netting.
A village is burning in the valley. In the watery light
smoke deepens over three hearthbeds of brightness.
A spire. A siding. A ladder of rooftops.
The gun fires. The picture trembles.

(Cut)

An iron darkening.
The hip of a tank blackens a frame,
foreshortened, the treads close to the lens,
a rushing of hammers, rings. The lens is cleared.
A cobbled street. A row of country-houses,
walled. A rosebush in the heavy light, blown
forward. Dust falls in the afterdraught,
a grain at a time. The camera is watchful.
A rifleman moves up the frame, his rifle at low port,
his shadow buffing the cobbles, crouched. He pauses
under the rosebush, his rifle hiked. A second figure
breaks through the frame, freezing between the
foreground and the far doorway. The man under
the rosetree sights carefully. The second man listens.
He raises his rifle, barrel backwards, and brings
the butt down heavily on the door panels.
The rifle rebounds.
He measures a second blow, his teeth bared
slightly in a reflex of anxiety. His eye is large.
The buttplate smashes over doorknob and lock,
the knocker flies upward once, the panel splinters
all at once. The man kicks the door open easily
with a booted foot. He listens, bent toward his
rifle-sights. He signals to the second man and enters
the doorway, stooped like a man entering a cave—

(Cut)

Brightness through trees. A damascene.
At the edge of a clearing, a parked jeep.
Two medical corpsmen lash litters to the jeep
engine a few hundred yards behind front lines.
The litter-poles enter the lens over the arch
of the engine. On the litter, a swathed head, a shock

134

of broken hair, motionless, a fall of blankets.
The stretcher-bearers vault lightly to their seats
and move off at a crawl.
Roadmarker: *Battalion Aid Station.* A corner of
charred wall, rubble, glass, timber. Legend: *Épicerie.*
The stretcher-bearers dismount.
The film is bad.
Presently a gloved hand in a surgeon's sheath,
holding a forceps. Briskly the hand moves over a
circlet of maimed flesh noosed in a bloody bandage.
A scalpel flashes between the living hand and the
human hurt, forcing the rind of the wound,
filling the frame. The camera submits, framing
the wound like a surgeon's retractor, its gaze
nerveless and saline. The gauzes blacken swiftly,
too heavy for the jaws of the forceps.
The surgeon at full figure. A breeze finds the fold
of his tunic. In the distance the litter-bearers are
leaning for the litter-poles. His eyes hold the optical
center of the lens, unanswered. His mouth rejects
contemplation, not yet relaxed. His hands are void
in their glimmering cicatrix of rubber.

The Casualty

(for David Schubert)

And have your answer out of your instinct's need
to render its terror tangible.

                              For howsoever shyly,
under the soldier's compulsion, with a human gaze,
puzzling disaster at a time when terror was usual,
you bent to the bullet a consented will—
you ripened volition with that other deed,
valor's improvisation, the unselving act,
to force an unspeakable image from the Maze.

Infantryman falling, falling always: your fall is forever.
Fall to your certainty, no longer compelled and alone,
yielding the gunstock to the compassionate image.
Turn from the bomb-burst by the powerless river
forfeit in crossfire, on inadmissive ground—
who have become that Host the night-march sought:
terror's unique enigma, the time-server's will,
the shield whereon Medusa's manifest gaze
glows like a boss and confronts its deliverer
in the bottomless pit and beast's face of the wound.

VI
The Five-Fold Mesh
(1938)

"Thou knowest this man's fall;
but thou knowest not his wrastling."
— Dorotheus

John Keats, Surgeon

"No, no: go not to Lethe . . ."

Surely the level shine of steel
Honed to the littleness of hair
Is implement enough to deal
A stroke to lay the spirit bare?

The hurt lies not so recondite
As point may drive or lancet bore—
Yet, though the blade drink long or light,
The fever kindles as before.

However the providential hand
Hew the division deep enough,
The sutures, though they tremble, stand,
And cast the kindly unguent off.

An upstart's quackery, at best—
To mitigate the lesser ill
And leave, like an unriddled jest,
The ruined heartbeat ailing still!

Is there a stranger provender
To get the ravaged part its peace—
Wolfsbane, aloe? Mandrake? Myrrh?

No, no: not these . . .

Charwoman: 20 Vesey Street

(Lower Manhattan—6:00 P.M.)

Clapping the door to, in the little light,
In the stair-fall's deepening plunge,
I see, in the slate dark, the lumped form, like a sponge,
Striking a rote erasure in the night—

And keep that figure, while a watery arc
Trembles and wanes in wetted tile, as if
It wrote all darkness down in hieroglyph
And spoke vendetta with a watermark.

That shadowy flare shall presently define
A scuffed and hazardous wrist, a ruined jaw
Packed into goiter like a pigeon's craw,
A bitten elbow webbed with a naphtha line—

While light shall lessen, blunting by brute degrees
The world's waste scanted to a personal sin,
Till all is darkness where her brush has been
And blinds the blackening marble by her knees.

*   *   *

I mark what way the dropping shaft-light went.
It flung the day's drowned faces out, and fell
Hasped like a coffin down a darkening well:

And poise on the shaft-way for my own descent.

(for Joseph Wood Krutch)

140

Early Testament

The quieter god comes early to the childhood
That is unhappy. There is space
In that sufficient shadow for the clasped hand and the wetted face,
The sackcloth in the burdock and the briar,
The outcry of the renegade denier:

Call

To the strong child-god, for He has ears
To pleasure the simple hunger, and He hears
The passage of our desultory tears:

> *"My child, my child,*
> *The feathers of my wings hang cool*
> *And all your tears are beautiful . . ."*

He was my friend. I never turned from Him.

Oh, never say:

"At length he turned from Me,
Flinging the frank flower from his brows, leaping the pleasant stream,
Darkening the sweet water with his shadow.
For some implausible dream
He left the congenial hills, left the good meadow,
Sowing the scorpion through the innocent wheat,
Hurting with his feet
The small, immeasurable grass
That would not let him pass . . ."

I had not stirred a limb
To turn from Him.
Most imperceptibly
I saw His vast loins girt and He was gone from me:

And so, when help was vain and He was very far,
Past the clasping of hands or the heart's call,
I hid my head
And wept for the betrayed, infatuate dead.

That is the truth and the whole truth and is all.

Battery Park: High Noon

1.

Suddenly the old fancy has me!

                         Suddenly,
Between flint and glitter, the leant leaf,
The formal blueness blooming over slate,
Struck into glass and plate,
The public tulips treading meridian glare
In bronze and whalebone by the statue-bases—
      Elude the Battery square,
          Turn with a southern gesture in remembered air
            And claim a loved identity, like faces . . .

2.

Compute the season out of height and heat.
Cubes in the poised shaft dwindle. Tackle moves.
Descending diners paddle into grooves
And burst from bolts and belts upon the street.

Summer deploys upon the brims of hats—
Turns upon twill; affirms with colored drinks
A mimic solstice poised in flying inks
In Babylons of ribbons and cravats.

Here thoroughfares are blind upon the sea.
Enter the packed paths where the lanes converge
That drop the derelict straggler by the surge
Like targets in a shooting gallery.

In middle sleep, below the list of bells
That turn soft answers to a barge's brass,
These take their length in quarantines of grass
Among the pigeons and the peanut shells.

Their capbrims crush out day. Fulfillments leap
Sudden as bludgeons in a vacuum.
They answer to the pricking of a thumb
And serve him more than slumber, who would sleep—

A stricter sleep I guess, with double dread,
Who waken now and dream these sleepers dead:

And yet, these are my dreams that dream the lie
And keep their sleep more deathfully than I.

Bend then to seaward. The element you ask
Rarer than sea is, wantoner than time.
You bear it on you strangely, like a mask,
And dream the sailing in a pantomime.

The element is blood. Tired voyager, turn.
The reckoning you take is yet to learn.
Somber, at fullest flood, the continents ride
And break their beaches in a sleeper's side.

3.

Follow the loll of smoke, fallow over water,
The expense of power in retentive stone
Where the barge takes the ripple with an organ tone—
Over water, over roof, over catchpenny green,
Into time-to-come and what-has-been:

> Into the chimney's well and the cistern's smother,
> Resin and amber shed on divided flame:
> Into the quick of the burning, combustion's vehement heart
> Flying the summery floor,
> Beating its pure pulse on the violet core—

> Into the million years' flowering . . . the ageless green . . .
> The sunken frond . . .
> The charmed marine . . .
> Time's incorruptible, biding, through char and pulp
> The ceaseless diamond.

O lost and mythic scene,
Move yet within this frame!
This is that angel, whether gem or flower,
Leaven and gum and flint,
Recalled from carbon in explicit power,
Whose massive slumber wears the pure impress
Of old renewal and first fruitfulness,
Pledging the fern's shape in primordial tinder,
Sealing, in herb and mint,
The healing in the cinder.

Measure again the ruinous floor of the world
Beyond the park-path and the seaward paling,
The equal faces, stunned with light and void,
Tranced as in surmise, lost between myth and mood,
Derelict, decoyed,
In some astonished dream of sailing . . .

The Enemy Joy

"Tarry, delight, so seldom met . . ."
—A. E. Housman

In jackal country, in the gum and umber,
That bird broke blank to the eyebeam.

                                She sprang
The feathery braid, the maze of slumber,
She trod the timeless humors, and the brief:
Her wings leapt thorny out of upper rain,
And chalked to stillness in that sparkling plane,
On derelict claws she sang.

    What heart's-ease and what thinking angers?

Her wings drove black on bright:
For pure delight
The cold throat like a lessening spindle shook.
She sang the enemy joy as it were grief
And, with a condor look,
A summer's space in blue
Bore down the wreath like rue.

                             (for Henry Roth)

Possessions

has been set by Dix Typesetting Company, Syracuse, New York, in a film version of Bulmer. The type was originally cut and designed by William Martin for Bulmer, one of the three figures most responsible for the English printing revival of the eighteenth century, and was used in the famous "Boydell Shakespeare" of 1791.

The book was designed by Virginia Evans and has been printed and bound by The Maple-Vail Book Manufacturing Group in Binghamton, New York.